FORTY DAYS OF PRAYER

SEVEN STEPS TO A SPIRITUAL BREAKTHROUGH

KIT CUMMINGS

About the author: Kit Cummings has taught these principles around the world in the toughest environments. Over the past decade Kit has served in over one hundred prisons, jails, detention centers, and rehab facilities and worked with over 10,000 inmates in some of the most dangerous areas of the world. In 2020, Kit received the NAACP *Living the Dream Award* for his contributions to civil rights and his work with at-risk youth and prison reform. He has journeyed on tours through Africa, Asia, Latin America, and Europe, and has authored six books including the award-

winning *Peace Behind the Wire, a Nonviolent Resolution*. Kit's latest book, *The New Convict Code*, flips the script on prison reform and aims to shatter the school to prison pipeline. For more information about his work and ministry go to www.KitCummings.com.

Theatron Press—*an imprint of Illumination Publishers*
www.ipibooks.com, 6010 Pinecreek Ridge Ct, Spring, TX 77379

Introduction

In 2004, after fifteen years in the fulltime ministry, I was burnt out and completely out of gas. Ministry had gone from being a calling to a career. It wasn't that I had lost my faith in God, or that I wasn't happy preaching anymore. It wasn't that I was no longer effective or that I couldn't grow a ministry. It wasn't that I had lost connection with my congregants or with our staff. I had simply stopped seeing the work of God in my life or in the lives of others. My relationship with God had grown stale, my relationships with the brothers in my life had become shallow, and I became disillusioned and bitter. The consequences of a lukewarm relationship with God began to show up. We really do reap what we sow. A marriage on the rocks and a strong pull from the world left me in a very vulnerable position, and I fell.

That season of life almost crushed me, but I found the strength to carry on and I set out to discover what had gone wrong and where the cracks in my spiritual foundation were. That desire sent me on an adventurous journey that continues to this day. A wonderful brother and friend gave me this charge and it changed my life: "Go out into the world and find out what God is up to and then come back and tell us." That's just what I did.

I went on a ten-year journey to explore where our Father was working the most powerfully, and I found him in very unexpected places. I found God in prisons, homeless shelters, youth gangs, rehabilitation facilities, and developing countries. I searched for him in synagogues, cathedrals, mosques, temples, ashrams, and sweat lodges. I've been in over a hundred prisons, jails, detention camps, homeless shelters, and recovery centers and seen amazing things. I've worked with over 10,000 inmates and over 10,000 teens, and they have changed my life forever. The "least of these" became my congregation and dirty tables became my pulpit.

After my fall, I was angry at all the wrong people, places, and things. I swore off churches and church people; I quit reading my Bible and stopped praying; and I began going to places I never should have been. Then one night, beaten into a state of reasonableness, I prayed a simple prayer that changed my life: "Father, if you ever see fit to let me preach again, which I do not expect, I will go to the harassed and helpless. I'll go to the hungry, the thirsty, the naked, the stranger, the sick, and the prisoner. Please don't be done with me yet." And that has made all the difference.

I set out to study and experience all the subjects and people that I had judged over all those years of religion. I studied cosmology and quantum mechanics; biology and psychology; philosophy and world religions; evolution and brain science. I met rabbis and imams; priests, medicine men, and shamans; gurus, yogis, and monks. Do you want to know what I found? After it was all said and done, I came back more in love with Jesus than I had ever been. I not only found my faith again, but a fire began burning inside me that has never died out and continues to get hotter to this day.

For several years after I resigned from the ministry, the last place I wanted to go was back to church, and I told God that I would never preach again. We tell God our plans and he laughs. I decided I would become a corporate motivational speaker and that's what I did, along with several jobs that could never fulfill me like preaching had done. Then my miracle arrived. I walked into my first prison in 2009 and something happened inside me. They weren't who I thought they'd be. They became my friends, and then they became my misfit band of brothers on the road to redemption. Ironically, prisons became my safe place, a place free from judgment and criticism. They became the church that I needed in order to heal. The least of these have incredible transformative power if you get close enough to catch it.

My fall from grace had been very public and God knew that I needed a private, safe place to heal. In his divine wisdom he chose the perfect spot for me. You see I had been through some suffering and lost some things, just like my brothers behind the wire had. I had faced ridicule, gossip, and shame, and so had they. I began to share things with them that you just can't share in church, and they loved me still. They laughed at my pain, in a good way, because they could identify. I found this magic in every prison I went to and in every homeless person I embraced. These hated, feared, and forgotten men became my comrades, my teachers, my consiglieres, and my guides. I didn't dare judge them because I remember what that felt like.

I had surely found what God was up to, and before long I was preaching about it; something I swore I would never do again. Be careful what you tell our Father. He remembered that promise I made about the harassed and helpless, and one night in tears I remembered it too. He was listening, he was working, and he brought it to pass in a way that I could never have imagined, and certainly in a way that I wouldn't dare take credit for. He took me to help the least of these in South Africa and Ukraine; Honduras, Guatemala and Mexico; India and all across America. Once I got hooked on this powerful ministry, I became bored with the traditional Christianity that I had practiced for years. I get hooked on whatever makes me feel good, and I got addicted to REAL. Once I had tasted that the Lord was good, I developed an insatiable thirst for more. The Spirit became my guide, and I continued to go where I was invited.

Somewhere along the journey I began to expect miracles and even started searching for them. I began to write down scary prayers and things that really challenged my faith, and I reviewed them daily. I started searching for God's fingerprints and evidence that he was working to bring about the miracles that I was seeking. I began journaling about the things I was seeing and learning. I started taking measurable steps toward the things that I was asking God to do for me. A momentum developed, and I began to pray for more and more miracles. I had seen God do amazing things in the most forsaken places, with the most forgotten people, and it changed the way that I saw everything and everybody.

I found a Father whom I had missed for all those years I was preaching, teaching, and counseling. I discovered a God who loves to play and loves to show me things through signs and wonders. No longer did I see a Lord who was upset with me when I disobeyed, or mad at me when I fell short. Instead, I saw my *Abba* pulling for me and helping me up when I slipped again. The Bible began to come alive as I saw Jesus and the way he treated people. How had I missed it? My prayer life became a grand game of hide and seek as I searched for more and more places where he was hiding. As he led me, I began to see him everywhere.

This led to the creation of my process which became this book. It worked so well for me that I decided to share it with the world. No one has seen the best work of my life, at least none of you have. God only allowed prisoners, gangsters, addicts, prostitutes, and beautiful homeless brothers and sisters to witness it. And I met some angels along the way as well. I believe that they hide among the least of these and watch how we treat them. In 2012, he told me to begin speaking about what I had seen and heard, and that is what I've done. I am about to release my sixth book, and it will not be my last.

He taught me to love without agenda, and with no strings attached. He taught me not to judge, but rather to look for God in people. He taught me to work with others who don't look like me, believe like me, or vote like me. He showed me that the last shall be first and that he is using the lowly, hated, and despised things of this world to shame the wise, just like he said he would. I do not regret the past nor do I wish to shut the door on it. Every single step of this crazy adventure has played a part, as has every mistake, and every individual that I have met along this unbeaten path. I wish the same for you.

Has your relationship with God gotten boring, tired, or heavy? Has the Bible become monotonous and rote? Has the church lost its fire and ability to inspire you? I'm here to tell you that there is hope. I'm a living, breathing example that God loves knuckleheads and he does his best work when we're broken and flat on our back. If he can use a drunken, fallen preacher like me, then he can certainly use you. If he can mobilize an army of faithful warriors behind the razor wire, then he can lift you up too. Your best days are most certainly ahead of you, if you're willing to try something new. If we keep doing the same things we've always done, then we'll keep getting what we always get.

Let's review the process and begin this miracle journey.

First, you'll commit to hitting your knees first thing every morning. This practice changed my life. I mean first thing. Roll out of your bed, onto your knees, and simply lift your eyes to God. This can be as short a prayer as you'd like, and then run to the bathroom! This simple act of submission sets the tone for your day and directs your energy and focus onto his power and not your own. This act is what many participants in this project say had the biggest impact on their life. I've been doing this for so many years I can't get out of bed any other way.

Next, you'll come up with ten impossible prayers, meaning they're impossible to do without divine power (you can come up with more than ten if you'd like). These should be prayers that scare you a little. They can involve your marriage or your kids; your health or your finances; your character or your courage; sin strongholds or forgiveness. These are things that you might have stopped believing are possible for you. Maybe you're afraid to get a broken heart if hope is deferred once again. It's not that you don't believe it's possible, but maybe you don't believe it's possible for you or yours. Here is my encouragement for you: a broken heart isn't so bad. I'd rather get my heart broken chasing my dreams than see it slowly break over years of disappointment and discouragement because I failed to stretch my faith.

Next, you'll review your miracle prayers every day and commit to praying for these things throughout your day. Don't pray in the morning and forget about them as you go about your day. Your father is ALWAYS working. This project is about seeing what he is doing on a daily basis. You'll learn to pray as you walk along, and as you sit down. You'll daydream about your miracles, and you'll imagine their arrival. This is what the Bible calls keeping in step with the Spirit. Talk to him and listen to him as you go along the path.

Next, you'll begin to take measurable steps toward your miracles every day. As you watch and pray, the Spirit will nudge you with thoughts, ideas, and answers, but you must move when he stirs you. When you have the thought to reach out to someone or to make a move on God's behalf, now is the time to act. Then you'll get deliberate about moves you can make to show God that you're paying attention. When you make one move, God makes two. Now you are gathering momentum.

Next, you will begin to journal regarding the evidence you find that God is working on your behalf. I call this searching for God's fingerprints. This is a huge part of the process. Over your forty days you will develop the habit of treasure hunting, as you look for God's reply to your requests and desires. Journaling is becoming a lost art, but it is so powerful when you practice it. I believe it becomes real to you when you write it down, and I think your Father likes it when it becomes real to you. As you record evidence you begin to search for more, and then you'll begin to notice him everywhere.

Next, you will keep your heart pure and soft by repenting as the Spirit shows you things along the way. It's not that God stops working when we fall, but rather we can't see him when our hearts are covered up and becoming hard through sin's deceitfulness. Keep your side of the street clean and you will begin to see him more clearly. When I am stuck in guilt or shame my eyes become focused on myself and I can no longer see others around me as clearly. Guilt can be a motivation, as it involves feeling bad about something I've done. However, shame is more destructive because it involves feeling bad about who I AM. Simply see the wrong and make it right. We can't allow shame to be a part of this game.

Next, you will begin the process of shifting back into a state of gratitude when you catch yourself complaining, blaming, or making excuses. These are all strategies for failure. These mindsets steal your power and take your eyes off of God and his work in your life. Gratitude in the midst of suffering is a powerful energy and keeps the flow wide open. When you develop a habit of gratitude you open up the floodgates of blessing into your life. When we focus on all the reasons that we are miserable we continue to find evidence of the same. What you focus on expands, and we find what we look for.

Lastly, at the conclusion of each week's study we will look at a series of powerful questions that Jesus asked people. Jesus brought out what was in people's hearts by asking great questions. This is the discussion portion of the project and great for families and small groups. Imagine Jesus asking you these questions as you plead with him to work in your life. These questions will uncover excuses and the things we hide behind when we get stuck.

If you'd like to put your prayer life on steroids, I recommend that you get a prayer partner for this endeavor. Accountability is very powerful when you desire it. You're attempting to break old habits that do not serve you and replace them with new ones. This is not easy, as your brain will stubbornly hold onto habits that you have developed over time. When you have someone in the battle with you it will give you strength when you feel like taking a day off from your spiritual training. If you're going to commit to this project, then do it with all your heart. Who knows, maybe your prayer partner needs you as much as or more than you need them.

You can also take it one step further. Get your family or small group to do this as a project. I also teach this as an eight-week spiritual breakthrough course for midweek services with small to medium-size congregations. This can wake up a sleeping church and start a fire with your ministry. Recently I have facilitated this training through Zoom with churches in South Africa including Pretoria, Johannesburg, and Durban. Technology allows us to connect all over the world. This is a prayer movement that you are becoming a part of.

I have recently begun a small group with a few brothers who are seeking miracles in different parts of the country. We call ourselves the Four Horsemen. Edi is in Alberta, Canada; John is in Winston-Salem, North Carolina; Jeff is in San Diego, California; and I am in Atlanta, Georgia. Every week we get on a Zoom call and discuss what God is doing in our lives and lean on each other for support. As we go through this project together again and again, we send each other short videos every day, and share what we got out of each day's devotional, and challenge one another. This process is bringing us close together and changing our lives. There is power in small groups.

One last word of encouragement: pay attention to the small miracles and don't give in to discouragement if you don't see God working on your impossible prayers. Most times I find that his answers don't come wrapped in the package that I expect. It is amazing when I find once again that he has answered another impossible prayer in a way that I never would have expected, or even noticed if I wasn't paying attention. As your impossible prayers are answered, circle them and blast them from the rooftops. Give him all the glory and encourage others to take the Forty Days of Prayer Challenge.

My prayer for you is that you will begin to SEE God in all his glory working for you every single day. "Delight yourself in him, and he will grant you the desires of your heart."

Peace to you and yours. Let us begin—miracles await.

For the next forty days I commit myself to the

Seven Point Prayer Pledge

1. I will get on my knees first thing every morning.

2. I will write out my impossible prayer list and review it daily.

3. I will pray for these things daily, and even hourly when needed.

4. I will take measurable steps toward my miracles every day.

5. I will watch and record "Miracle Sightings and Spiritual Insights" and the evidence of God's work in my life daily.

6. When I am wrong, I will promptly admit it and quickly make amends.

7. I will deal with my doubts, excuses and complaints diligently and faithfully, and choose gratitude instead.

To begin each day, read aloud the following prayer and commit it to memory:

Lord, make me an instrument of your peace.
Where there is hatred, let me sow love.
Where there is injury, pardon.
Where there is doubt, faith.
Where there is despair, hope.
Where there is darkness, light.
Where there is sadness, joy.

O Divine Master,
Grant that I may not so much seek to be consoled,
* as to console;*
To be understood, as to understand;
To be loved, as to love.
For it is in giving that we receive.
It is in pardoning that we are pardoned,
And it is in dying that we are born to Eternal Life.

—attributed to St. Francis of Assisi

As your impossible prayers are answered share them with others to encourage them to *believe* and participate!

My 40 Day Impossible Prayer List

1) _____

2) _____

3) _____

4) _____

5) _____

6) _____

7) _____

8) _____

9) _____

10) _____

"Have faith in God," Jesus answered. "Truly I tell you, if anyone says to this mountain, 'Go, throw yourself into the sea,' and does not doubt in their heart but believes that what they say will happen, it will be done for them. Therefore I tell you, whatever you ask for in prayer, believe that you have received it, and it will be yours. And when you stand praying, if you hold anything against anyone, forgive them, so that your Father in heaven may forgive you your sins."

—Mark 11:22–25

Let's begin moving some mountains...

Luke 11:1–13

One day Jesus was praying in a certain place. When he finished, one of his disciples said to him, "Lord, teach us to pray, just as John taught his disciples."

He said to them, "When you pray, say: "'Father, hallowed be your name, your kingdom come. Give us each day our daily bread. Forgive us our sins, for we also forgive everyone who sins against us. And lead us not into temptation.'"

Then Jesus said to them, "Suppose you have a friend, and you go to him at midnight and say, 'Friend, lend me three loaves of bread; a friend of mine on a journey has come to me, and I have no food to offer him.' And suppose the one inside answers, 'Don't bother me. The door is already locked, and my children and I are in bed. I can't get up and give you anything.' I tell you, even though he will not get up and give you the bread because of friendship, yet because of your shameless audacity he will surely get up and give you as much as you need.

"So I say to you: Ask and it will be given to you; seek and you will find; knock and the door will be opened to you. For everyone who asks receives; the one who seeks finds; and to the one who knocks, the door will be opened.

"Which of you fathers, if your son asks for a fish, will give him a snake instead? Or if he asks for an egg, will give him a scorpion? If you then, though you are evil, know how to give good gifts to your children, how much more will your Father in heaven give the Holy Spirit to those who ask him!"

—Jesus

Pledge One Reminder

1. I will get on my knees first thing every morning.

These seven steps set me free from a legalistic prayer life and helped me build a true relationship with God and the Holy Spirit. Each week I will review one of the seven steps and reinforce why they are so powerful and potentially life changing. I encourage you to review the steps each day. Whichever one of the steps you are struggling with, simply ask yourself why, without judgment, and reset with new resolve. We can do anything for forty days, why not give it a try?

At the end of each round of this forty-day project we take time for the participants to share their most powerful takeaways. The one step that has produced the most dramatic results for most people is this simple but powerful practice. In 2012 I started rolling out of bed onto my knees and I never stopped. I've been doing it for so long I can't get out of bed any other way!

Most people use their phone as their alarm clock these days. When it goes off and you pick it up, you naturally look to see what's on it. Has someone texted me? Do I have any new emails that are urgent? Did I miss any calls, or is there anything on social media that I need to check in on? The day hasn't even begun and the world is already pulling at you. Once you check your phone, use the restroom, brush your teeth, get your coffee, talk to your spouse, kids or roommates, check the news and get situated, your mind is already filled with information and the voice in the head has begun to speak. Based on the quality of the information you have consumed since your first waking thoughts, the trajectory of your day is set, and your habits are reinforced.

This one simple step changes all of that. Through repetition, you will form a new habit that intentionally sets the tone for your day. When you roll out of bed, seamlessly onto your knees, you are immediately brought into a posture of submission. Your first waking thoughts, of the 50,000 you will have that day, are directed toward your Father, and your first words are uttered to Him and only Him. It doesn't matter how long you stay in that position or how many words you speak, the point is to wake up and immediately connect with God before the outside world has already gotten your attention. This is your first intentional act of devotion and God has truly gotten your first fruits.

Obviously, if you have any health issues that make this difficult or impossible for you, then you can adjust to create your own unique habit. If you practice this powerful step for forty days in a row your brain will begin to rewire itself and before long you will be doing it unconsciously. Prepare yourself, this first step is a game-changer!

Day One
Genesis 15:1–6

After this, the word of the LORD came to Abram in a vision:

"Do not be afraid, Abram.
I am your shield,
your very great reward."

But Abram said, "Sovereign LORD, what can you give me since I remain childless and the one who will inherit my estate is Eliezer of Damascus?" And Abram said, "You have given me no children; so a servant in my household will be my heir."

Then the word of the LORD came to him: "This man will not be your heir, but a son who is your own flesh and blood will be your heir." He took him outside and said, "Look up at the sky and count the stars—if indeed you can count them." Then he said to him, "So shall your offspring be."

Abram believed the LORD, and he credited it to him as righteousness.

We might as well start where faith for many began. Three world religions and almost two thirds of the world's population look back to this man's faith...Abraham is forever known as the Father of Faith. Why? Because he *believed* God. Period. And that belief led to action. Abraham and Sarah were well past the years for child bearing. This was definitely miracle territory. He was trusting God to do something that seemed impossible and outside the norm, simply because God had promised. Sarah laughed at the notion, but Abraham dared to believe beyond what was visible and "realistic." And look what came from that **one** act of faith. There were dozens of reasons for him not to believe, so much evidence against this crazy idea, and plenty of opportunity for him to talk himself out of getting his hopes up.

What is your "impossible" prayer to God? What have you given up on? What seems unrealistic and unreasonable to ask him? Do you have the kind of relationship with your Father where you can dare to ask him for things that are far beyond reason or your typical experience? Begin your *Impossible Prayer List* today, and stretch yourself. Write down things that scare you a little. God gave Abraham a son at the age of 100! But first he had to believe that God had the power to do what he said he would. Imagine what God can accomplish in your life, if you will only ask and *believe*. "Is anything too hard for the Lord?" Hit your knees and stretch your faith. Look up at the stars...your journey of faith has begun.

Miracle Sightings and Spiritual Insights

_____

_____

_____

_____

_____

_____

_____

_____

_____

_____

_____

_____

Day Two
Genesis 18:22–25

> The men turned away and went toward Sodom, but Abraham remained standing before the LORD. Then Abraham approached him and said: "Will you sweep away the righteous with the wicked? What if there are fifty righteous people in the city? Will you really sweep it away and not spare the place for the sake of the fifty righteous people in it? Far be it from you to do such a thing, to kill the righteous with the wicked, treating the righteous and the wicked alike. Far be it from you! Will not the Judge of all the earth do right?"

We are **all** interconnected. One blessing impacts another, and every curse has a ripple effect. We have no idea how our faith can affect another. Abraham had a heart for people, and not just his own people. He also had the kind of relationship with God in which he felt like he could reason with him and try to persuade him. God didn't mind this. God had a special place in his heart for his son and he encouraged Abraham to "work things out" with him. Who do you have in your life that desperately needs intercessory prayer? Someone is fighting for their spiritual life and they need *you* to reason with God on their behalf (perhaps they're too weak to fight on). Add them to your *Impossible Prayer List* and pray specifically for their deliverance *every* day. Praying for others adds special power to your personal prayer life as well. Watch for evidence that the circumstances are about to change because of *your* faith. Don't be afraid to remind God of his promises—he seems to encourage that. Consider bringing this person into your journey as a prayer partner for the next six weeks. Who knows, it may very well change both of your lives forever.

Miracle Sightings and Spiritual Insights

_____

_____

_____

_____

_____

_____

_____

_____

_____

_____

_____

_____

_____

_____

_____

_____

_____

_____

_____

_____

_____

_____

Day Three
2 Chronicles 14:11

> Then Asa called to the Lord his God and said, "Lord, there is no one like you to help the powerless against the mighty. Help us, O Lord our God, for we rely on you, and in your name we have come against this vast army. O Lord, you are our God; do not let man prevail against you."

Sometimes we feel as though we are facing insurmountable odds and defeat seems imminent. There is a vast army coming against us and our backs are against the wall—however, you must remember, God *is* that "wall." What is the "impossible" battle that you are facing right now in your life? Is it a financial concern, a health issue, marital problems, kids in trouble, or a spiritual crisis? It is time to run back into that battle, but with a newfound faith. These are the areas of our lives that wear us down and take away our courage over time. Call on God to come to your rescue, and do not be afraid to bring *his* honor into it, as Asa did. Is your God bigger than your problem, or does your problem seem bigger than God? Certainly it is not. The battle lines have been drawn and the enemy is shouting across the lines at you. Your God is just waiting to rush into the fray on your behalf. Call on God and stand up to the "enemies" in your life. Now go and *look* for your answer from God!

Miracle Sightings and Spiritual Insights

_____

_____

_____

_____

_____

_____

_____

_____

_____

_____

_____

_____

_____

_____

_____

_____

_____

_____

_____

_____

_____

_____

_____

_____

_____

Day Four

Matthew 8:5–8, 13

When Jesus had entered Capernaum, a centurion came to him, asking for help. "Lord," he said, "my servant lies at home paralyzed, suffering terribly."

Jesus said to him, "Shall I come and heal him?"

The centurion replied, "Lord, I do not deserve to have you come under my roof. But just say the word, and my servant will be healed."

Then Jesus said to the centurion, "Go! Let it be done just as you believed it would." And his servant was healed at that moment.

This Roman gentile had a faith that astonished Jesus and was more pure and powerful than that of the people of God. He understood how power in the "real world" worked and he reasoned that things worked similarly in the faith world. The fact that he understood and *trusted* the authority of Jesus turned Jesus' head and got his attention—and he was a gentile "sinner"! Do you wish to astonish Jesus today? Pray something that you have never dared or even dreamed of praying. Claim the authority of Jesus over an area of your life that has been a "thorn" in your side, an impossible stronghold that all the normal tactics have not succeeded in dismantling. He has all the power—we must call on *his* authority to remove that stronghold. Clearly identify the problem; then hold it up to the power of Jesus and his authority. Look at your *Impossible*

Prayer List and pray through it with the divine power to demolish strongholds. Go! It will be done just as *you* believe it will. That's a blessing or a curse, depending on *your* faith.

Miracle Sightings and Spiritual Insights

Day Five
Acts 4:29–31

> "Now, Lord, consider their threats and enable your servants to speak your word with great boldness. Stretch out your hand to heal and perform signs and wonders through the name of your holy servant Jesus."
>
> After they prayed, the place where they were meeting was shaken. And they were all filled with the Holy Spirit and spoke the word of God boldly.

Persecution and opposition had come to the apostles because of their fearless stand for the truth. Is there an area of your life that is under attack simply because you refuse to compromise, give in or submit to peer pressure? What you need is *divine boldness*. The apostles were already acting boldly in the name of the Lord, but now they needed divine intervention to take them to the next level. Maybe you're doing pretty well. Why not go to a place that you've never been before spiritually? Participate in an "earth-shaking" prayer. God loves it when you call on him in strength, not just when you are out of other options. Go to a special place with a trusted friend, where you can shout to the Lord and call on him to act on your behalf in regard to your Impossible Prayers. Two are better than one and there is spiritual power in numbers. Call on God together to consider spiritual threats and obstacles and enable you to be even *bolder*! Most times you'll find that after you pray in faith, those threats are just "imposter bullies" that need to be challenged. Fear and faith cannot occupy the exact same space and time. Simply replace your fear with faith through *bold prayers*. Now you have a prayer partner to walk with as you continue this six-week journey of miracles.

Miracle Sightings and Spiritual Insights

_____

_____

_____

_____

_____

_____

_____

_____

_____

_____

_____

_____

_____

_____

_____

_____

_____

_____

_____

_____

_____

Day Six
Acts 10:1–4

> At Caesarea there was a man named Cornelius, a centurion in what was known as the Italian Regiment. He and all his family were devout and God-fearing; he gave generously to those in need and prayed to God regularly. One day at about three in the afternoon he had a vision. He distinctly saw an angel of God, who came to him and said, "Cornelius!"
>
> Cornelius stared at him in fear. "What is it, Lord?" he asked.
>
> The angel answered, "Your prayers and gifts to the poor have come up as a memorial offering before God."

God continually watches and searches throughout the earth for people who are not only praying, but walking by faith and showing their faith by what they *do*. Once again, God uses the faith of a gentile as an example for his chosen people. Cornelius not only feared God and prayed regularly, but he gave generously to those in need. Have you fallen into the habit of begging God for something in the morning and then walking out the door and forgetting completely what you prayed about? Today you need to remember that God is watching your good deeds, and he responds quickly and powerfully to those who combine faith with *action*. Do something selfless for someone in need today—someone who cannot repay you. Take the time to *see* the people that God puts in your pathway. You'll be amazed to see that God answers so many of our prayers through what appear to be random encounters with complete strangers. Sometimes you'll see that he even uses angels if you pay close enough attention. The people you will meet today are not merely distractions or hindrances, but rather messengers and opportunities. See God's hand in everything you do today. Now, go and *look* for your answer from God, but look for it in the eyes of the people that come into your path.

Miracle Sightings and Spiritual Insights

Day Seven
Luke 23:39–43

> One of the criminals who hung there hurled insults at him: "Aren't you the Messiah? Save yourself and us!"

> But the other criminal rebuked him. "Don't you fear God," he said, "since you are under the same sentence? We are punished justly, for we are getting what our deeds deserve. But this man has done nothing wrong."

> Then he said, "Jesus, remember me when you come into your kingdom."

> Jesus answered him, "Truly I tell you, today you will be with me in paradise."

I cannot wait to meet this man (traditionally known as Dismas) in heaven. What an amazing finish to a possibly wasted life. I do not know if this man was a career criminal or just had a bad day, but I know that he must be one of the most grateful individuals of all time! What if he had just thought it and never opened his mouth? What if he had talked himself out of asking and just given up instead? What if he thought he knew how Jesus was going to answer and didn't waste his time—and been terribly wrong? (We make terrible "fortune tellers," by the way.) But he didn't. He asked the right question to the *only* one who could give him what he truly desired. And for those who think that they are not "good enough" to ask God for help in a particular area, just ask Dismas. He wasn't a good guy either. Are you willing to ask God? Stop talking yourself out of your miracle. Ask him out loud. Stop thinking you already know what he'll say. Ask him again, and again. Ask him until you *find* your miracle. You have no idea what he might do for you until you try. Just ask Dismas!

Miracle Sightings and Spiritual Insights

_____

_____

_____

_____

_____

_____

_____

_____

_____

_____

_____

_____

_____

_____

_____

_____

_____

_____

_____

Week One Discussion

John 5:1–10

Some time later, Jesus went up to Jerusalem for one of the Jewish festivals. Now there is in Jerusalem near the Sheep Gate a pool, which in Aramaic is called Bethesda and which is surrounded by five covered colonnades. Here a great number of disabled people used to lie—the blind, the lame, the paralyzed. One who was there had been an invalid for thirty-eight years. When Jesus saw him lying there and learned that he had been in this condition for a long time, he asked him, "Do you want to get well?"

"Sir," the invalid replied, "I have no one to help me into the pool when the water is stirred. While I am trying to get in, someone else goes down ahead of me."

Then Jesus said to him, "Get up! Pick up your mat and walk." At once the man was cured; he picked up his mat and walked.

The day on which this took place was a Sabbath, and so the Jewish leaders said to the man who had been healed, "It is the Sabbath; the law forbids you to carry your mat."

THE QUESTIONS OF JESUS

Week One Discussion: *"Do you want to get well?"*

When people came to Jesus with requests and pleas for help, he often asked them a simple question. He asked not because he didn't know the answer, but rather to see if the individual asking understood the heart of the matter. The questions of Jesus revealed what was in the heart of the person asking for help.

In this encounter Jesus wanted to know if the paralytic wanted to get well. That is an interesting question, as a matter of fact it kind of feels like a foolish question. At first glance you would think the answer was a resounding YES. However, if we dig a little deeper, we find that the paralytic, upon receiving his blessing (new legs), used those legs to take him to a place he shouldn't have been. We know this because Jesus finds him the next day and says, "See, you are well again. Stop sinning or something worse might happen to you."

So maybe he is asking you now, "Do you really want to get well?" It's a very good question. Getting well carries responsibilities. Perhaps Jesus expected the man to use his new legs to serve the less fortunate in the place that he had laid paralyzed for thirty-eight years. Maybe he will expect you to use your blessing for his purposes as well.

Think about what you are asking of Jesus, and then ask yourself the same question: "Do I really want to get well? Am I ready to use the blessing he gives me to help others?" If you allow him to heal you, then there is work to do.

Week One Topics and Questions

- How has getting on your knees first thing every morning changed your prayer life?

- Do you really want to get well? Share the reasons why.

- Discuss the signs that accompany a person who truly wants to be healed.

- Discuss the reasons why someone might want to

stay in their misery rather than being healed, and the excuses one might use to stay in their current condition.

- Discuss the responsibilities that come along with getting well.

_____

_____

_____

_____

_____

_____

_____

_____

_____

_____

_____

_____

_____

_____

_____

_____

_____

_____

_____

_____

Pledge Two Reminder

2. I will write out my impossible prayer list and review it daily.

This step radically changed my life. After years of ministry my prayer life had become routine and had gotten dull and monotonous. I needed a seismic shift in my relationship with God. My prayers were very general and vague and I tended to pray about the same things, in the same way, at the same time, in the same place. Can you relate? So I added one simple element: I began to write my impossible prayers down and became very specific about the things I was asking my Father to help me with.

When we write something down, whether it be a goal, a to-do list, or a prayer, it becomes real. If I review the things that I am praying for daily my brain gets locked in and begins to unconsciously search for those things on my behalf. The more specific the better. The brain is designed by God to notice and bring my attention to the things that it has learned are important to me. The more specific the prayer, the more the brain begins to search. It's like Google. If you give it the right keywords it will find exactly what you're asking for. If you stay general and vague in your prayer life how will you know when His answers show up?

So I began to get very specific with what I was praying for and began to review those things every day, and even began to practice imagining their arrival. Some are not willing to do this because they are afraid that God won't answer their prayers and they will be crushed once again. Many of us have been hurt because we prayed and prayed about a certain thing or person and never found the answer. So maybe we learn to pray "safe" prayers so that we won't get our hearts broken again. I made a bold decision not to worry about my heart being broken again. Heart breaks are a part of life, and for the most part, I have no control over these things. I'd rather get my heart broken chasing my dreams than slowly let it grow cold praying weak, superficial prayers that have no power.

Get very specific and write down things that scare you; the things that you've given up on over the years. Risk a broken heart and pray for the impossible. You'll be amazed at what you begin to see. God loves it when we get REAL with Him.

Day Eight

Daniel 9: 20–23a

> While I was speaking and praying, confessing my sin and the sin of my people Israel and making my request to the LORD my God for his holy hill—while I was still in prayer, Gabriel, the man I had seen in the earlier vision, came to me in swift flight about the time of the evening sacrifice. He instructed me and said to me, "Daniel, I have now come to give you insight and understanding. As soon as you began to pray, a word went out, which I have come to tell you, for you are highly esteemed."

How encouraging is that!? As Daniel began to pray, God sent Gabriel *immediately* with an answer (and he hadn't even finished the prayer!). Imagine the angels standing before God awaiting their assignments, and then Daniel begins to pray, and his prayers enter the throne room. "Gabriel, attention!" Now, stop before you explain it away and say, "Well, that was Daniel, and that was way back then." Why would God work that way then and not for you now? He is not trapped in space and time and he sees it all laid out before him, so there is no "back then versus nowadays" in the spiritual realm. Is it perhaps because we don't *believe* he works like that anymore? You are highly esteemed: Pray through your *Impossible Prayer List* on your knees, out loud, and visualize angels "in flight" immediately with an answer. God is on the edge of his throne waiting to see some impossible faith! Angels are ministering spirits sent to serve *us*. They are ready, willing and able to work as God directs them. Get them involved in your good fight, and then go and *search* for his reply. Attention, Gabriel!

Miracle Sightings and Spiritual Insights

_____

_____

_____

_____

_____

_____

_____

_____

_____

_____

_____

_____

_____

_____

_____

_____

_____

_____

_____

_____

_____

_____

Day Nine

2 Samuel 7:18–22

> Then King David went in and sat before the LORD, and he said:
>
> "Who am I, Sovereign LORD, and what is my family, that you have brought me this far? And as if this were not enough in your sight, Sovereign LORD, you have also spoken about the future of the house of your servant—and this decree, Sovereign LORD, is for a mere human!
>
> "What more can David say to you? For you know your servant, Sovereign LORD. For the sake of your word and according to your will, you have done this great thing and made it known to your servant.
>
> "How great you are, Sovereign LORD! There is no one like you, and there is no God but you, as we have heard with our own ears."

David's gratitude produced a deep humility in his prayer life. He felt as though he was the luckiest man on the planet—and think of all that he had been through! He honestly believed that God had taken special care of him and that he was truly a "favored son." David had committed some of the worst sins imaginable, yet God called him a man after his own heart. Do you feel like that? I have seen firsthand some of the most impoverished people in the world with some of the most amazing attitudes of gratitude. Spiritual blessings many times have nothing to do with worldly possessions or physical attributes. Do you want to put your prayer life on steroids? Find your gratitude. Make a list today of all the blessings in your life, *before* you begin to pray. It doesn't need to be long, but it certainly can be. However, it needs to be genuine and sincere. Meditate on all that God has done for you and how richly he has blessed you. Now, in that powerful, grateful energy, remembering how he has answered you in the past, present your requests to God. Pray *bold,* impossible, miraculous prayers with deep, humble, rich gratitude to the King of Kings! Remember that he has proven himself faithful time and time again, and be *sure* that he is answering these prayers too, even as you are praying them. Gratitude opens the door for blessings to flow into your life.

Miracle Sightings and Spiritual Insights

Day Ten
Psalm 51:10–13

Create in me a pure heart, O God,

    and renew a steadfast spirit within me.

Do not cast me from your presence

    or take your Holy Spirit from me.

Restore to me the joy of your salvation

    and grant me a willing spirit, to sustain me.

Then I will teach transgressors your ways,

    so that sinners will turn back to you.

David is praying for a "pure heart" during a true, heartfelt prayer of repentance. Listen to what he desires from his Father: purity, steadfastness, presence, joy, willingness, sustenance and selflessness. Wow. Now, why would God *not* answer a prayer such as this? Sometimes it's easy to rationalize seemingly unanswered prayers by saying: "It must not be his will." But we know that God wants us to have a pure, steadfast, joyful, willing, powerful, selfless heart. Many times we spend all of our prayer time asking God to change our external circumstances, rather than to change our internal attitudes. So today, why not implore God to create in you a *new* heart, and truly believe that he is busy molding it and shaping it and will give you every single, specific thing you need today to refine it, test it and strengthen it. Now today if you encounter situations that frustrate you, just remember this prayer and trust that God is doing *exactly* what you asked him to do. Pray it now, and go and *look* for God's answer. And don't be surprised if it shows up in a "package" that you do not expect! God loves to answer our prayers in ways that we would least expect (but you must be paying attention to catch it). Humble yourself and *he* will lift you up!

Miracle Sightings and Spiritual Insights

James 5:13-18

> Is anyone among you in trouble? Let them pray. Is anyone
> happy? Let them sing songs of praise. Is anyone among
> you sick? Let them call the elders of the church to pray
> over them and anoint them with oil in the name of the Lord.
> And the prayer offered in faith will make the sick person
> well; the Lord will raise them up. If they have sinned, they
> will be forgiven. Therefore confess your sins to each other
> and pray for each other so that you may be healed. The
> prayer of a righteous person is powerful and effective.
>
> Elijah was a human being, even as we are. He prayed
> earnestly that it would not rain, and it did not rain on the
> land for three and a half years. Again he prayed, and the
> heavens gave rain, and the earth produced its crops.

Imagine the prayer life of a man so powerful that he
produced a three-and-a-half-year drought—and then called
in the rain again! And here is the convicting part: He was a
man just like us. He was tempted, he got sick, he got scared,
he had times of weakness and sin, he strayed and he was just
like us—he didn't always feel like a hero. One small difference:
genuine faith. Do you feel like you have to be perfect to have
your prayers answered? Do you feel powerless if you haven't
confessed all of your sin? Do you feel weak and timid when
you are in trouble, sick or wounded? Elijah can relate. And
yet God answered his Impossible Prayer and changed his
circumstances. Perhaps you have something on your heart that

is stealing your joy: a guilty conscience, a nagging ailment or an injury or a stubborn doubt; then by all means pick up the phone and find some "agreement" from your prayer partner. Find strength on your knees with a trusted friend—the idea is to pray over your problem. It's time to call down the *rain*. Open up the floodgates of your faith. Ask God for something that's a real stretch. He loves it when we call on him in the midst of the storm, or in the heat of a raging battle, or in the middle of a faith "drought." He can handle it. Can you muster up the faith today? All it takes is a mustard seed. Just ask Elijah.

Miracle Sightings and Spiritual Insights

Day Twelve
1 Kings 17:20–22

> Then he cried out to the LORD, "LORD my God, have you brought tragedy even on this widow I am staying with, by causing her son to die?" Then he stretched himself out on the boy three times and cried out to the LORD, "LORD my God, let this boy's life return to him!"
>
> The LORD heard Elijah's cry, and the boy's life returned to him, and he lived.

Once again we find a prayer warrior who was so confident in his relationship with God that he wasn't afraid to respectfully question God's seemingly apparent will. He boldly questioned God and pleaded with him to change his mind. We have no idea if this was God's will all along and if he had planned on raising the boy from the start; but we see the heart of Elijah and his love for the widow's son. His first instinct was to believe that God could do anything, and he wasn't afraid to ask. He believed in his all-powerful, all-knowing, all-present, all-loving Creator and Sustainer of life. Was anything too hard for him? Is there an area of your life or a "decision" that you think that God has made that you need to recommit to overturning? There are definitely things that God, in his infinite wisdom, decides that can never be changed or amended; but this is a forty days of *miracles* project, and I bet there is an area or a concern that you can reignite with faithful fire. Find your passion and begin to discuss it with your Father, respectfully, but fervently once again. Who knows what is possible? It's time to give it a valiant effort. Elijah gave a woman back her son. Perhaps God will give *you* back your courageous heart.

Miracle Sightings and Spiritual Insights

Day Thirteen
2 Kings 6:17–18

> And Elisha prayed, "Open his eyes, LORD, so that he may see." Then the LORD opened the servant's eyes, and he looked and saw the hills full of horses and chariots of fire all around Elisha.
>
> As the enemy came down toward him, Elisha prayed to the LORD, "Strike this army with blindness." So he struck them with blindness, as Elisha had asked.

This is one of my all-time favorite episodes in the Bible. Elisha had learned from his mentor Elijah's powerful prayer life, and now he was passing it on to his servant. They were in a seemingly hopeless situation—completely surrounded by the enemy on every side and totally outmanned and outnumbered. Do you ever feel that way? What was the servant's problem? His lack of vision. He could not see what Elisha could see, because he wasn't looking with eyes of *faith*. When God opened his eyes, he immediately saw that the situation was not as it seemed. The truth was that God's army had the enemy vastly outnumbered with chariots of fire! It wasn't even close. Today, I want you to look at your biggest problem, your greatest fear and your best excuse with eyes of faith, rather than fear. If you cannot accomplish this on your own, then just imagine how a fearless and faithful prayer warrior would look at your situation—then borrow some of their faith in the same way that Gehazi borrowed faith from Elisha. Call your prayer partner and ask them how you both will choose to look at the situation today. Pray a *bold* prayer, then open your eyes and look at your circumstances from a different perspective. There is more than one way to look at every challenge. And remember, he has you surrounded with a ring of fire.

Miracle Sightings and Spiritual Insights

_____

_____

_____

_____

_____

_____

_____

_____

_____

_____

_____

_____

_____

_____

_____

_____

_____

_____

_____

_____

_____

_____

Day Fourteen

Judges 6:12-18

When the angel of the Lord appeared to Gideon, he said, "The Lord is with you, mighty warrior."

"Pardon me, my lord," Gideon replied, "but if the Lord is with us, why has all this happened to us? Where are all his wonders that our ancestors told us about when they said, 'Did not the Lord bring us up out of Egypt?' But now the Lord has abandoned us and given us into the hand of Midian."

The Lord turned to him and said, "Go in the strength you have and save Israel out of Midian's hand. Am I not sending you?"

"Pardon me, my lord," Gideon replied, "but how can I save Israel? My clan is the weakest in Manasseh, and I am the least in my family."

The Lord answered, "I will be with you, and you will strike down all the Midianites, leaving none alive."

Gideon replied, "If now I have found favor in your eyes, give me a sign that it is really you talking to me. Please do not go away until I come back and bring my offering and set it before you."

And the Lord said, "I will wait until you return."

Gideon, the "mighty warrior" hiding in a wine press. The smallest, the weakest, the lowliest in his clan—at least in his *own* eyes. Do you ever feel that way? Where are all this power, strength and the mighty wonders that he promised and that everyone else seems to be experiencing? Where is *your* blessing? We can all relate to Gideon at some time or another: hiding, complaining, excusing and blaming, with all God's power at our disposal at this very moment. However, Gideon wanted some proof from God that he *really* was with him—and God didn't mind him asking for it. I love that about my God. He isn't ashamed of our weakness, our struggles, our failures or our doubts; but he does expect us to deal with them. Today, maybe you need to ask him for a "sign." Don't be afraid—ask him to show himself to you. But now you must go and search for the sign. That's where many people fall short. They pray and then forget to watch. Look for signs in the people you meet today, the things you happen to notice along the way, and the random coincidences that are woven into the fabric of your daily walk. Go in the strength that you have today...you mighty warrior.

Miracle Sightings and Spiritual Insights

_____

_____

_____

_____

_____

_____

_____

_____

_____

_____

Week Two Discussion
Matthew 20:29–34

As Jesus and his disciples were leaving Jericho, a large crowd followed him. Two blind men were sitting by the roadside, and when they heard that Jesus was going by, they shouted, "Lord, Son of David, have mercy on us!"

The crowd rebuked them and told them to be quiet, but they shouted all the louder, "Lord, Son of David, have mercy on us!"

Jesus stopped and called them. "What do you want me to do for you?" he asked.

"Lord," they answered, "we want our sight."

Jesus had compassion on them and touched their eyes. Immediately they received their sight and followed him.

THE QUESTIONS OF JESUS

Week 2 Discussion: *"What do you want me to do for you?"*

These men just wanted to see, so they shouted for Jesus to have mercy on them. Jesus appears to love giving people their sight. He seems attracted to the blind. Maybe it's because it so dramatically changes our life when we go from blindness to sight. This project is all about changing the way we see things, or perhaps to see some things you've never seen before.

Once again Jesus asks a question that seems obvious. They were blind and were seeking mercy, but Jesus still wanted to know exactly what they desired from him. Have you been specific with your impossible prayers, or are you still staying vague and general, remaining in a "safe" place spiritually? Jesus wants to know what you really believe you need from him.

Imagine Jesus coming to your village and asking you the same question. If you had one shot to ask him anything, what would it be? What is your ONE thing? You know, the thing that, if healed, would take you to a place you've never been before. That's the question that he wants you to ask. Don't waste your shot, ask him and be very specific.

Week Two Topics and Questions

- How has writing down your specific prayers changed your prayer life?

- What exactly do you want Jesus to do for you?

- Discuss why plans typically succeed when we get specific but tend to fail when we keep things general and vague.

- Discuss why we might be afraid to get specific regarding the things that we want to change in our lives, and why we are oftentimes unwilling to write them down.

- Discuss why we have a hard time sharing our dreams and goals publicly in front of our family, friends, and fellow church members.

Pledge Three Reminder

3. I will pray for these things daily, and even hourly when needed.

Have you ever gotten into the habit of praying for things in the morning and then forgetting what you prayed about as you go about your day? All of us have. That is why I added this step. As I began writing down my prayers, and reviewing them every day, they became stuck in the forefront of my mind. As I meditated and imagined their arrival, I found myself expecting to find my answers. The more I focused on what I really desired and needed, the more I began to carry those requests in my heart and on my mind as I went along. Jesus said to "Watch and pray." For years I had been praying but not watching, and I was missing everything. This one step brought faith back into my walk. The Holy Spirit began to guide me like a spiritual GPS, and I began to really listen.

God knows what we need before we ask Him, and that's why He told us not to waste words like the Pharisees and the pagans who do not know God. He knows what we should be talking to Him about, but sometimes we talk about everything except the ONE thing that we really need His help with. Praying for the same things in the same way every day made me dull, and when I'm dull, I forget what is important. I made this book pocket-sized so that I could carry it along as I went. I began to remember the things I was searching for and then continued to pray for them as I went. I developed a walking prayer life, and my relationship with God became a wonderful treasure hunt and an exciting game of hide-and-seek. I found that His answers were everywhere, I just hadn't been paying attention.

If need be you can always set reminders on your phone and take time throughout the day to stop and focus on your impossible prayers. You'll be amazed what you'll find when you open your eyes and your ears and begin to pay attention.

Day Fifteen
1 Samuel 1:10–16

In her deep anguish Hannah prayed to the LORD, weeping bitterly. And she made a vow, saying, "LORD Almighty, if you will only look on your servant's misery and remember me, and not forget your servant but give her a son, then I will give him to the LORD for all the days of his life, and no razor will ever be used on his head."

As she kept on praying to the LORD, Eli observed her mouth. Hannah was praying in her heart, and her lips were moving but her voice was not heard. Eli thought she was drunk and said to her, "How long are you going to stay drunk? Put away your wine."

"Not so, my lord," Hannah replied, "I am a woman who is deeply troubled. I have not been drinking wine or beer; I was pouring out my soul to the LORD. Do not take your servant for a wicked woman; I have been praying here out of my great anguish and grief."

Sometimes our prayer life is dark and sad and even feels lonely. Sometimes we feel like no one can understand our grief or pain. Maybe it's something that has happened; maybe it's someone we've lost, or maybe it's something we really want or need. And sometimes we just need to weep. God is moved by tears and deep heart sadness. He hears your prayers, even if you can't get them out of your mouth—like Hannah: Her mouth was moving, but nothing was coming out. It's OK. Just pray however you need to pray. He *knows* what you need and even what you desire before you ask him. Let it out, however you need to. Some of the most important times of my spiritual life were times of ugly, angry and even bitter prayers that I had to get out. And God answered me still. Hannah made a vow, which sometimes can be very powerful and life-changing. Be very mindful about vows, and I would encourage you to seek wise counsel, but get it out and begin to wrestle with your God. Don't be afraid to go into that dark place. Take a trusted friend if need be. Hannah got her baby and fulfilled her vow—and God will answer your Impossible Prayer today too.

Miracle Sightings and Spiritual Insights

_____

_____

_____

_____

_____

_____

_____

_____

_____

_____

_____

_____

_____

_____

_____

_____

Day Sixteen
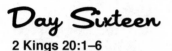

2 Kings 20:1–6

> In those days Hezekiah became ill and was at the point of death. The prophet Isaiah son of Amoz went to him and said, "This is what the LORD says: Put your house in order, because you are going to die; you will not recover."
>
> Hezekiah turned his face to the wall and prayed to the LORD, "Remember, LORD, how I have walked before you faithfully and with wholehearted devotion and have done what is good in your eyes." And Hezekiah wept bitterly.
>
> Before Isaiah had left the middle court, the word of the LORD came to him: "Go back and tell Hezekiah, the ruler of my people, 'This is what the LORD, the God of your father David, says: I have heard your prayer and seen your tears; I will heal you. On the third day from now you will go up to the temple of the LORD. I will add fifteen years to your life."

It seemed as though God had made up his mind again. It was time to call Hezekiah home. We all have our "time" to go; and God is the one who decides. But Hezekiah wasn't ready to go yet. He had work left to do. Once again we see someone with the bold, impossible *faith* that feels confident to reason with God about his divine will. Very few would have even had the thought, much less the guts to give it a shot! Most would've talked themselves out of it, even if they did have a crazy thought like that—to attempt to change God's mind about the time of a man's own death? I think God liked it. And he gave him fifteen more years. Now we all know that God determines the times and the places, and many times even the circumstances, of our lives, but don't you just love these men and women who had the courage to get "outside the box" and cry out to God for him to do something *very* unusual? What do you need to ask God to do for you? What is your Impossible Prayer? Maybe you need to go back and really take a hard look at your *Impossible Prayer List* again—but this time look at it like Hezekiah would. I bet he treasured those fifteen years. I bet he'd tell us that he is so glad he had the courage to ask. I bet he is pulling for you to follow his lead (even though he wasn't perfect—or especially because he wasn't).

Miracle Sightings and Spiritual Insights

_____

_____

_____

_____

_____

_____

_____

_____

_____

_____

_____

_____

_____

_____

_____

Day Seventeen

Romans 8:26–27

> In the same way, the Spirit helps us in our weakness. We do not know what we ought to pray for, but the Spirit himself intercedes for us through wordless groans. And he who searches our hearts knows the mind of the Spirit, because the Spirit intercedes for God's people in accordance with the will of God.

This is one of the most encouraging scriptures in the whole Bible to me. Even when, and especially when, I do not know what to pray for, the Spirit is praying earnestly and specifically on my behalf. He knows *exactly* what I need, when I need it, and just how to get it to me. Period. Always. Every time. So today if you aren't really sure what you should pray about, just sit quietly and stare at your *Impossible Prayer List* and listen for the Spirit's voice. Get very still and meditative and just *listen*. He will pray *for* you—all you need to do is be present and hear his still, quiet voice. But also know that sometimes he is shouting in words and groans that you can't even fathom! Sometimes he is asking God to do specific things and arrange certain circumstances in ways that make absolutely no sense to us—and he knows exactly what he is doing, especially when we don't. God understands his own voice and is already on his way. Believe that today.

Miracle Sightings and Spiritual Insights

_____

_____

_____

_____

_____

_____

_____

_____

_____

_____

_____

_____

_____

_____

_____

_____

_____

_____

_____

_____

_____

_____

_____

_____

_____

Day Eighteen

1 Chronicles 4:9–10

> Jabez was more honorable than his brothers. His moth-
> er had named him Jabez, saying, "I gave birth to him in
> pain." Jabez cried out to the God of Israel, "Oh, that you
> would bless me and enlarge my territory! Let your hand
> be with me, and keep me from harm so that I will be free
> from pain." And God granted his request.

This is a fascinating, obscure little passage that became
famous in a small book that was published years ago. Jabez,
who we know fairly little about, was on his way to leaving a
"legacy of pain." Even his name meant pain! However, God
considered him more honorable than his brothers. Something
in his life, his heart, his walk—something—just stood out. And
he inquired of the Lord. He prayed for something that many
would talk themselves out of: "That's selfish. That's all about
me. That's probably not his will. That's just not humble." Do
you ever feel that way? That you're not allowed to pray for
comfort, less harm, less pain, prosperity, abundance and a
larger territory? Less *pain*? Well, Jabez did. And God answered
him and gave him less pain, less harm, more comfort and a
larger inheritance—his Father's hand was upon him and he
changed his legacy forever. The obvious key is to live honorably
today, but also to ask for your heart's desire and for God's will
to be done in your life. Ask boldly, ask often, ask again—and
walk as though your boundaries have been *enlarged* and

expanded today. "Acting" humble doesn't make you humble. Just act honorably and let God worry about the property lines.

Miracle Sightings and Spiritual Insights

Day Nineteen
Genesis 32:24–28

> So Jacob was left alone, and a man wrestled with him till daybreak. When the man saw that he could not over-power him, he touched the socket of Jacob's hip so that his hip was wrenched as he wrestled with the man. Then the man said, "Let me go, for it is daybreak."
>
> But Jacob replied, "I will not let you go unless you bless me."
>
> The man asked him, "What is your name?"
>
> "Jacob," he answered.
>
> Then the man said, "Your name will no longer be Jacob, but Israel, because you have struggled with God and with humans and have overcome."

Talk about a life-changing prayer time: Jacob not only got a new name, but changed the course of a nation. We have no idea how many lives are changed by just *one* answered prayer. But first we must ask. Sometimes we must persist. And every now and then we must *wrestle* with God. I believe that like any good parent, our perfect Father sometimes wants to see how bad we want something. We need to wrestle in order to build our character. We need to battle to refine our inner core. We need the times of testing to find out who we are and what we're made of. If you squeeze a lemon, you get lemon juice. Squeeze a man, and you find out what is on the inside of that man. Jacob learned a lot about himself that night: He was much tougher than he realized. Are you willing to roll up your sleeves and get dirty, maybe even a little "bloody" today to get what you really want? Some aren't willing to pay the price; I believe that you are. Wrestle through your *Impossible Prayer List* today with a renewed strength, some determination and an iron resolve. Show God what you're made of. And just maybe you'll learn a little something about yourself too—maybe you'll even get a new name.

Miracle Sightings and Spiritual Insights

Day Twenty

Jeremiah 1:4–10

The word of the LORD came to me, saying,

> "Before I formed you in the womb I knew you,
>
> before you were born I set you apart;
>
> I appointed you as a prophet to the nations."

"Alas, Sovereign LORD," I said, "I do not know how to speak; I am too young."

But the LORD said to me, "Do not say, 'I am too young.' You must go to everyone I send you to and say whatever I command you. Do not be afraid of them, for I am with you and will rescue you," declares the LORD.

Then the LORD reached out his hand and touched my mouth and said to me, "I have put my words in your mouth. See, today I appoint you over nations and kingdoms to uproot and tear down, to destroy and overthrow, to build and to plant."

Jeremiah made a tremendous impact on this world, but he was given a very challenging ministry. God called him when he was young, appointed him, equipped him and then *sent* him. Jeremiah would endure much suffering and incredible pain because of his love for his people, his faith in God and the calling that his Father had placed on his life (he would forever be known as the Prophet of Tears). Do you ever feel a glorious burden that you believe God has placed on your life? Do you feel called to do something great but also feel totally inadequate? Jeremiah can relate to you. I wonder if he ever regrets answering God's call from where he sits today—I seriously doubt it! He found his place, made his impact, and left a powerful legacy. He had *one life*, and he used it all up, living life to the full—even in pain. You could do that. But first you must be honest with God about how you feel. The same weak, rehearsed prayers every day have not done the trick. It's time to get honest with God and let him know your concerns, your fears, your doubts and your weakness and inadequacies. Tell him the truth, but then be prepared to respond to his call anyway—God loves to work "in spite of." Not tomorrow, but today. Today is the day to answer his call. Do something today that you've never done before. Pray a *bold* prayer for strength, and then go and find your answer from God today. (Are you seeing a pattern here?)

Miracle Sightings and Spiritual Insights

_____

_____

_____

_____

_____

_____

_____

_____

_____

_____

Half-time Locker Room Speech

1 Kings 19:1–13

Now Ahab told Jezebel everything Elijah had done and how he had killed all the prophets with the sword. So Jezebel sent a messenger to Elijah to say, "May the gods deal with me, be it ever so severely, if by this time tomorrow I do not make your life like that of one of them."

Elijah was afraid and ran for his life. When he came to Beersheba in Judah, he left his servant there, while he himself went a day's journey into the wilderness. He came to a broom bush, sat down under it and prayed that he might die. "I have had enough, LORD," he said. "Take my life; I am no better than my ancestors." Then he lay down under the bush and fell asleep.

All at once an angel touched him and said, "Get up and eat." He looked around, and there by his head was some bread baked over hot coals, and a jar of water. He ate and drank and then lay down again.

The angel of the LORD came back a second time and touched him and said, "Get up and eat, for the journey is too much for you." So he got up and ate and drank. Strengthened by that food, he traveled forty days and forty nights until he reached Horeb, the mountain of God. There he went into a cave and spent the night.

And the word of the LORD came to him: "What are you doing here, Elijah?"

He replied, "I have been very zealous for the LORD God Almighty. The Israelites have rejected your covenant, torn down your altars, and put your prophets to death with the sword. I am the only one left, and now they are trying to kill me too."

The LORD said, "Go out and stand on the mountain in the presence of the LORD, for the LORD is about to pass by."

Then a great and powerful wind tore the mountains apart and shattered the rocks before the LORD, but the LORD was not in the wind. After the wind there was an earthquake, but the LORD was not in the earthquake. After the earthquake came a fire, but the LORD was not in the fire. And after the fire came a gentle whisper. When Elijah heard it, he pulled his cloak over his face and went out and stood at the mouth of the cave.

Then a voice said to him, "What are you doing here, Elijah?"

We are at the midway point, and I just wanted to encourage you. Here we find Elijah, the great prophet, hiding, complaining, making excuses and feeling quite the victim. And then he had a little talk with Jesus. God's answer was not in the earthquake, the fire or the mighty wind, but in a gentle whisper. God works in mysterious ways, and you might not find his answer at first glance. You've got to hang in there and finish the second half in order to accomplish your "great comeback." Don't allow yourself to get discouraged and give up. The glory is in the getting up, the rising again and the great comeback in the second half. God is gently asking you: "Why are you here?" To find our *miracle*, that's why.

Now let's dig in again...

Day Twenty-One

Matthew 11:25–26, 28–30

> At that time Jesus said, "I praise you, Father, Lord of heaven and earth, because you have hidden these things from the wise and learned, and revealed them to little children. Yes, Father, for this is what you were pleased to do.

> "Come to me, all you who are weary and burdened, and I will give you rest. Take my yoke upon you and learn from me, for I am gentle and humble in heart, and you will find rest for your souls. For my yoke is easy and my burden is light."

Congratulations! You are three weeks into your miraculous journey of faith. By now, if you have been fighting this good fight *every* day, you might feel a little weary and burdened and in need of some rest. Perfect. That is how Jesus must have felt every day—but he continued to draw his strength from his Father as he continued to pour himself out. That is why he withdrew and prayed so often, so fervently and so consistently—he knew he needed to in order to recharge and renew. I also believe that the reason Jesus loved children so much, and the reason they were so drawn to him, was because he was childlike. He had the faith of a child, the purity of a child and the imagination of a child—with the mind and heart of God. Children seem to have unlimited energy, like they are tapped directly into the Source. Hopefully over the last few weeks you have begun to see God do some things that you have never seen him do or haven't seen him do in a long time. Now is the time to dig down deep, go to him and find the strength to carry on. If you do *anything* for forty days, new patterns, pathways and habits are formed. Imagine what will become of you if you continue to pray boldly and to search for your answers *every* day, but through the eyes of a child: with raw energy and enthusiasm. It will become a way of life—I promise. Just don't give up five minutes before you see God move in your life.

Miracle Sightings and Spiritual Insights

Week Three Discussion
Matthew 9:27–31

As Jesus went on from there, two blind men followed him, calling out, "Have mercy on us, Son of David!"

When he had gone indoors, the blind men came to him, and he asked them, "Do you believe that I am able to do this?"

"Yes, Lord," they replied.

Then he touched their eyes and said, "According to your faith let it be done to you"; and their sight was restored. Jesus warned them sternly, "See that no one knows about this." But they went out and spread the news about him all over that region.

THE QUESTIONS OF JESUS

Week 3 Discussion: *"Do you believe I am able to do this?"*

Once again Jesus is asked to grant sight to the blind. However, this time he responds with a different question. "Do you believe that I am ABLE to do this?" This is a very important question.

The reason I call my prayer requests "Impossible Prayers" is to remind myself that these are things that I cannot accomplish without his help. As you review your specific prayers every day it is important to bring this question to mind. Jesus wants to know if you believe that he has the power to bring about the miracles that you seek.

We are seeking divine intervention and the power to demolish strongholds during this six-week journey. Whether your issues revolve around health, finances, relationships, sin strongholds, or character defects, we must believe that Jesus can do for us that which we cannot do for ourselves. So, the question for you is: Do YOU believe that he is able to bring about YOUR miracle?

Week Three Topics and Questions

- How have you taken steps toward your impossible prayers this week?

- Do you really believe that Jesus is able to bring about the miracles you are seeking?

- Discuss how our past failures play a role in our willingness to believe whether or not God can work in our lives today.

- Discuss a time in your life when you wanted something so badly that you were willing to go to great lengths to attain it.

- Discuss a miracle from your past that proved to you that God was intervening on your behalf.

_____

_____

_____

_____

Pledge Four Reminder

4. I will take measurable steps toward my miracles every day.

This step put my prayer life on steroids. I discovered that I had been sitting back and waiting for God to answer my prayers without personally getting involved in the action. I decided that for me this was faith without deeds, which are basically "dead" prayers. If I am asking God to get involved, to intervene, to overturn, to amend, or to create something out of nothing, then He expects me to act as if I believe that He is on His way.

So I began making moves in the direction of the miracles that I was seeking. As I reviewed my impossible prayers in the morning, and meditated on what their arrival might look like, invariably ideas would pop into my mind that would speed their coming. Whether the prayer was about health, finances, marriage, forgiveness, kids, ministry, or sin strongholds, I began to think of ways that I could show God that I was believing what I was praying. I began to act "as if" it was already given and create an action step in the direction of my heart's desire. Faith WITH deeds is powerful and effective, and I began finding the fruit.

This forty-day project is going to change the energy of the word "miracle." I used to think as though that word only applied to red sea crossings or Lazarus coming out of the grave. Of course those are indeed biblical miracles, but I began to see all of God's work as miraculous. Albert Einstein said, "Either everything is a miracle or nothing is. I choose the former." When God intervenes on my behalf and brings about the impossible, I call that a miracle. The Creator Himself is getting involved in human affairs and doing for me that which I cannot do for myself.

Make a move in the direction of the miracle you are seeking. You take one step and your Father will take two. Your next move might show up in the form of an idea, an epiphany, or a revelation. It might be a slight "nudge" from the Holy Spirit as He brings someone or something to your mind. The key is to make a move when you sense the nudge. Pay attention and you will begin to hear Him speak.

Day Twenty-Two
John 11:38–44

> Jesus, once more deeply moved, came to the tomb. It was a cave with a stone laid across the entrance. "Take away the stone," he said.
>
> "But, Lord," said Martha, the sister of the dead man, "by this time there is a bad odor, for he has been there four days."
>
> Then Jesus said, "Did I not tell you that if you believe, you will see the glory of God?"
>
> So they took away the stone. Then Jesus looked up and said, "Father, I thank you that you have heard me. I knew that you always hear me, but I said this for the benefit of the people standing here, that they may believe that you sent me."
>
> When he had said this, Jesus called in a loud voice, "Lazarus, come out!" The dead man came out, his hands and feet wrapped with strips of linen, and a cloth around his face.
>
> Jesus said to them, "Take off the grave clothes and let him go."

This has to go down as one of the most amazing comebacks of all time. Do you need a comeback in your life? Lazarus was dead for *four days*. There was a smell. There were mourners. There had already been a funeral. It was *over*. Then Jesus showed up. He prayed out loud for the benefit of his hearers, but he didn't need to. He knew that his Father always heard *and* answered his prayers—always. So why would this time be any different? Because the stakes were higher, or the odds more stacked, or the chances were seemingly less for victory? None of that mattered to Jesus. All that mattered was the will of God. And so Jesus asked, or more specifically, he declared what was to be. What is the area of your life that is over? Whether it be your marriage, your children, your career or lack thereof, your personal righteousness, your health, a wound, or any other "mountain" that is in your way; what you need is for Jesus to arrive. As Mary had stated: "Lord, if you had been here, my brother would not have died." At least she knew that the presence of Jesus made all the difference. Ask Jesus to "show up" in the most desperate area of your life—today (and don't begin to talk yourself out of it with excuses and evidence from the past). But after you pray, you must do something as well: You must take off the grave clothes. You cannot pray your Impossible Prayer this morning and then walk out the door and live as though you are in mourning because you do not believe that he is with you. *If* you believe, you *will* see the glory of God.

Miracle Sightings and Spiritual Insights

_____

_____

_____

_____

_____

_____

_____

Day Twenty-Three
Matthew 26:36–39

> Then Jesus went with his disciples to a place called Gethsemane, and he said to them, "Sit here while I go over there and pray." He took Peter and the two sons of Zebedee along with him, and he began to be sorrowful and troubled. Then he said to them, "My soul is overwhelmed with sorrow to the point of death. Stay here and keep watch with me."
>
> Going a little farther, he fell with his face to the ground and prayed, "My Father, if it is possible, may this cup be taken from me. Yet not as I will, but as you will."

Here we see Jesus in his weakest moment. He needed his Father, but he also needed his brothers. He was about to face something that he had never faced. The emotional, mental, physical and spiritual anguish was almost too much for him to bear. He got through it alone, with his Father, but he also asked for help from his friends—and he was not ashamed to show weakness. We should ask for help from our friends more often. Many are going through their toughest time or their darkest hour, right now. Be it emotional, physical, mental, financial or spiritual, you've made it this far. Valiantly perhaps, you've gotten through it all alone—just you and your Father. However, you could use a friend to help carry the load. Call your prayer partner or a trusted friend today and share your *Impossible Prayer List* with them. Set up a time to cry out to God together, and "agree" on what you're asking of him. Two are better than one, and *anything* we ask in his name, believing, will be done for us. When two or more gather in his name and ask in faith, miracles happen. Ask for whatever you need and also pray for *his* will to be done. Jesus found the strength to do his Father's will—especially when it was contrary to his feelings. And don't forget that you can also help carry the load for another. You'll be amazed at the power that will flow into your life when you carry a heavy load *together*.

Miracle Sightings and Spiritual Insights

Day Twenty-Four
Luke 23:33–34

> When they came to the place called the Skull, they cruci-
> fied him there, along with the criminals—one on his right,
> the other on his left. Jesus said, "Father, forgive them, for
> they do not know what they are doing." And they divided
> up his clothes by casting lots.

This is perhaps the most amazing and powerful prayer
in the Bible: Jesus praying for his killers *as they were killing
him.* Wow. Unforgiveness is a powerful energy and a very
destructive force. It leads to resentment, bitterness and
eventually disillusionment. When we pray fervently for things
that we need but harbor resentment, jealousy and bitter envy in
our hearts, we should not be surprised when we lack spiritual
power and do not find what we seek. Today if you are really
serious about finding answers from God, begin by cleaning up
your side of the street. Make sure that there is no resentment
or grudge in your heart getting in the way of your *Impossible
Prayer Life.* Jesus reminded us to lay down our gift, go and get
right with our brother, *then* go and present our gift at the altar.
Go ahead and pick up the phone. Call that brother, sister, friend
or family member. Say you're sorry or say, "I forgive you." Don't
wait until the feelings come, because they might not. Just pick
up the phone and open the flow. Then watch what happens
to your prayer life. You will experience newfound power and
focus. You will begin to see things that you have been missing.

You will *find* your miracle. Don't put it off another day; maybe your friend needs it even more than you do.

Miracle Sightings and Spiritual Insights

_____

_____

_____

_____

_____

_____

_____

_____

_____

_____

_____

_____

_____

_____

_____

_____

_____

_____

_____

_____

_____

_____

_____

_____

Day Twenty-Five

Luke 23:44–46

> It was now about noon, and darkness came over the whole land until three in the afternoon, for the sun stopped shining. And the curtain of the temple was torn in two. Jesus called out with a loud voice, "Father, into your hands I commit my spirit." When he had said this, he breathed his last.

In the middle of the day complete darkness consumed the land. The temple curtain was torn in two from top to bottom. A powerful earthquake broke apart the rocks, and tombs were split wide open. The most powerful and world-changing event in all of human history was happening, as mankind was killing the "light of the world." And Jesus prayed a simple prayer: "Into your hands I commit my spirit." I trust you; I know that you've *got* me; all I have is you; please don't forget me; I need you; nothing else matters now; I'm betting everything on *you*; catch me as I fall.... What if you had that simple attitude today? What if you were able to stay in the moment, not obsess about yesterday or tomorrow, and just completely *trust* him? Do you believe that he is trustworthy? Can you really put *all* your cares on him? That is what we are attempting to do together for this *40 Days of Prayer Project*. Take your impossible situations and totally give them over to him. Put aside whatever has or hasn't happened in the past, and forget for a moment what might happen tomorrow; and just trust him today. Stop blaming everyone else for your problems and just put your entire focus on God and what he is doing right now in your life. Can you do that? Give it a try, and now look over that *Impossible Prayer List* again and realize that the clouds are breaking and the Light is on his way.

Miracle Sightings and Spiritual Insights

_____

_____

_____

_____

_____

_____

_____

_____

_____

_____

_____

_____

_____

_____

_____

_____

_____

_____

_____

_____

_____

Day Twenty-Six
Job 42:2–5

"I know that you can do all things;
> no purpose of yours can be thwarted.

You asked, 'Who is this that obscures my plans without knowledge?'

> Surely I spoke of things I did not understand,
> things too wonderful for me to know.

"You said, 'Listen now, and I will speak;
> I will question you,
> and you shall answer me.'

My ears had heard of you
> but now my eyes have seen you."

Job came to understand and respect God in a whole new way through life circumstances, interactions with his friends and open, honest dialogue with his Father. That is *exactly* what we are attempting to do over these forty days: to come to understand that God will have his way; that nothing is impossible for him; that he created *all* things, and he can do whatever, with whomever, however and whenever he chooses. And we need to deal with our friends and family and understand how influential we are with one another—for both good and bad. You might have some people in your life that support you in every way. You might also have some folks around you that are not exactly crazy about the discovery of miracles in your life. Today I want to challenge you to *see* God in everything. See him in the sunrise; see him in the wildlife; see him in the eyes of your children; see him in the technology that he has enabled us to create and utilize; see him in the laughter you hear at the office; see him in those who oppose you; see him in the love of your spouse; see him in the sunset; see him all through the sights, sounds, smells, tastes and feelings of your entire day—but please make sure to *see* him. Now remember that you are praying to the same God who created all of this and can do with it whatever he pleases. There are mountains of evidence for you to *believe*. Follow the example of Job and repent of your unbelief. And if need be, change the people you are surrounding yourself with—their influence can be very powerful in your life.

Miracle Sightings and Spiritual Insights

_____

_____

_____

_____

_____

_____

_____

_____

_____

_____

_____

Day Twenty-Seven
Jonah 2:1–2, 7

From inside the fish Jonah prayed to the LORD his God.
He said:

"In my distress I called to the LORD,
and He answered me.
From deep in the realm of the dead I called for help,
and you listened to my cry.

"When my life was ebbing away,
I remembered you, LORD,
and my prayer rose to you,
to your holy temple."

Let's take a fresh new look at your *Impossible Prayer List*.
Let's look at it from a different angle; a different perspective;
a different vantage point. Let's look at it from inside the belly
of a huge fish! There have been actual reports of fishermen at
sea in the modern era surviving after being swallowed by giant
fish (one story even claims that the acid inside the fish burned
off the fisherman's hair and took the pigment from his skin,
which might explain Jonah being a "sign" to the people!) Now,
having hopefully suspended some of the doubt as to whether
or not this could really happen, let's imagine Jonah crying out
from "inside" this impossible situation. All hope was gone. He
had no other options. No one could come to his rescue and all
other resources had been exhausted. Can you relate to him?
When was the last time you went somewhere where you could

really cry out to God? I mean let it *all* out with yells, cries, tears if necessary, and no worries about what anyone would think. Maybe you need a special place out in the middle of nowhere, where you can go when you need to have one of those special times with your Father. Pick a spot that is significant for you and is symbolic of "miracle territory" when you desperately need a breakthrough. Go to that spot and make it unique and personal for your prayer life. Go ahead and shout. Raise your voice and be *heard* from inside your unique situation. He doesn't need you to, but sometimes it helps *us* to break through spiritual belly walls, bone and cartilage in our lives. And know this: God hears you as your cries come up before his throne in his holy temple. Listen; you can hear the echoes.

Miracle Sightings and Spiritual Insights

Day Twenty-Eight
Joshua 10:7–8, 12–13

So Joshua marched up from Gilgal with his entire army, including all the best fighting men. The LORD said to Joshua, "Do not be afraid of them; I have given them into your hand. Not one of them will be able to withstand you."

On the day the LORD gave the Amorites over to Israel, Joshua said to the LORD in the presence of Israel:

"Sun, stand still over Gibeon,
and you, moon, over the Valley of Aijalon."

So the sun stood still,
and the moon stopped,
till the nation avenged itself on its enemies

I love the fact that Joshua even had the idea to pray this bold, outlandish prayer! Who would have even thought about it, much less given it a shot? I imagine how it must have impressed God when he heard Joshua ask for him to stop the **sun** so that he could have more time to fight for his people. I bet Jesus was astonished; he might have even stood up from his throne! Now, what can you do today to get his attention? You know you already have his undivided attention, but how can you astonish him with an Impossible Prayer today? Just imagine where this day took Joshua's faith and his relationship with God. I bet it blasted him into a stratosphere of faith the likes of which he had never seen. When we begin to walk by faith again, we will want the day to last longer so that we can continue to fight the good fight, not like the masses that cannot wait for the day to end. Don't talk yourself out of your miracle, your healing, your rescue or your bailout. God *is* listening, and he is waiting to hear what you have to say. Pray for extra energy, more enthusiasm and more strength of heart today as you seek God's will for your life. Stop watching the clock waiting for your day to be over, and start looking for God to amaze you—just maybe you'll start noticing "extra time."

Miracle Sightings and Spiritual Insights

_____

_____

_____

_____

_____

_____

_____

_____

_____

_____

_____

_____

_____

_____

_____

_____

_____

_____

Week Four Discussion
Luke 8:22–25

One day Jesus said to his disciples, "Let us go over to the other side of the lake." So they got into a boat and set out. As they sailed, he fell asleep. A squall came down on the lake, so that the boat was being swamped, and they were in great danger.

The disciples went and woke him, saying, "Master, Master, we're going to drown!"

He got up and rebuked the wind and the raging waters; the storm subsided, and all was calm. "Where is your faith?" he asked his disciples.

In fear and amazement they asked one another, "Who is this? He commands even the winds and the water, and they obey him."

THE QUESTIONS OF JESUS

Week 4 Discussion: *"Where is your faith?"*

Storms reveal the quality of our faith. If you want to know how you're really doing spiritually, check your pulse in the midst of a storm. A dangerous squall is what we find in this story. The disciples were fishing, like they had done so many times before. However, on this day they encountered a storm unlike any they had ever been through. Life is like that; it shows up on its own timing, on its own terms, and it doesn't ask permission.

The brothers had been with Jesus for a while at this point and they had seen amazing things. He was doing things that no one had ever done before, and they were on the front row for his miracles. However, when this storm rolled through, they lost their minds. They woke him up from a dead sleep and challenged him: "Don't you care if we drown!" Amazing.

His response came in the form of another question. He didn't get upset, and he didn't blast them. He simply asked, "Where is your faith?" Right in the middle of the battle, we need to ask ourselves the same question. "Where is my faith right now?" Maybe you feel like he is sleeping while the battle rages around you. He isn't. He is quite aware of what you are going through. Keep moving forward, it's time to find your faith in the storm.

Week Four Topics and Questions

- How has journaling and recording miracle sightings changed your prayer life?

- Where is your faith today? Make an honest assessment.

- Discuss what true faith looks like and how you know when it is present.

- Discuss how the storms of life have revealed the quality of your faith.

- Discuss the recent storms in your life that have damaged your faith, and how you can look at them differently going forward.

Pledge Five Reminder

5. I will watch and record miracle sightings and spiritual insights and the evidence of God's work in my life daily.

This whole project is about removing the scales from our eyes so that we can see what our Father is already doing all around us. It's all about vision and seeing God in the details of our lives. This step is where things started to get really exciting. I began to actively SEARCH for evidence that God had already answered my prayers and I began asking Him for signs to point me in the right direction. I called the evidence that I found "God's Fingerprints" and I became the investigator.

As I directed my attention to Him first thing in the morning; as I got really specific and wrote down the things I was seeking; as I carried those things with me throughout the day without forgetting what I was looking for; and as I began making moves in the direction of the miracles I was seeking, a fascinating momentum began to develop. I began noticing things that I had been missing when I was stuck in a boring, shallow prayer life. It turns out His fingerprints were everywhere. All this time He had been working, just as Jesus said He would, but I wasn't paying attention and I was blaming Him for not answering my prayers!

Are you comfortable asking your father for signs? Gideon did it, and God didn't seem to mind. I ask Him for signs all the time, and I have learned to pay attention. I ask for open doors and I ask for closed doors; I ask for the Holy Spirit to speak to me; I ask for Him to guide my steps toward my answers; and I ask my Father to show me things to let me know that I'm on track and going where He wants me to go. He always responds, every single time, without fail. You can count on that.

I began to write down and record the fingerprints I was finding and the signs that God had shown me the day before. In the morning after I review the steps and my impossible prayer list, I think back over the day before and bring to mind all the little things that happened that encourage me that my miracles are on their way. It could be a random text or phone call, or an idea that comes to mind that is the answer I have been seeking. It could be running into an old acquaintance at just the right time or finding an open door that reveals itself through an unexpected invitation. The more that I wrote down the things I was noticing, the more God continued to reveal Himself. Before long I was seeing Him EVERYWHERE. Pay attention, you'll be amazed what you begin to see when you look through eyes of faith. And give Him a wink every now and then to let Him know that you SEE Him.

Day Twenty-Nine
Matthew 8:1–3

> When Jesus came down from the mountainside, large crowds followed him. A man with leprosy came and knelt before him and said, "Lord, if you are willing, you can make me clean."
>
> Jesus reached out his hand and touched the man. "I am willing," he said. "Be clean!" Immediately he was cleansed of his leprosy.

We know from history and the Jewish culture during this period that this man was an outcast, an exile, a "less than" and a throwaway... yet he felt as though Jesus might not only accept him, but possibly make him clean. "Clean" would mean he could be accepted in society again. Clean meant that he could perhaps have his family back. Clean meant that he could go wherever he wanted, with whomever, any time he wished—true freedom. Can you relate to him in any way? Do you ever feel like you have been left behind, shut out or kicked aside? Or maybe you're experiencing some of the early signs of spiritual "leprosy." The first symptom of this terrible disease is a lack of feeling. Once the feeling starts to leave, then the body begins to break down. There are many people who are wearing the name Christian today, but they just don't feel anything anymore. Studying, praying and church attendance just doesn't seem to do it for them like it once did; the emotion has gone completely out of it. They need a miraculous healing.

The most important question you can ask is: "Lord, are you *willing* to make me clean?" You must believe that Jesus is not only able, but he is willing. You can be clean again. Imagine the freedom that awaits you. Imagine how this former leper felt as he ran, shouted and leapt through town sharing the good news about what Jesus had done for him. That could be you. But first you've got to go to the Great Physician and tell him what hurts. Pray for a healing of your heart, and then go live life today knowing that he is *always* willing and that you are truly free.

Miracle Sightings and Spiritual Insights

Day Thirty
Exodus 8:8–10

> Pharaoh summoned Moses and Aaron and said, "Pray to the LORD to take the frogs away from me and my people, and I will let your people go to offer sacrifices to the LORD."
>
> Moses said to Pharaoh, "I leave to you the honor of setting the time for me to pray for you and your officials and your people that you and your houses may be rid of the frogs, except for those that remain in the Nile."
>
> "Tomorrow," Pharaoh said.

I want you to imagine frogs *everywhere*. Frogs in the streets, in the fields, in the houses—even in your bed! This plague was one of the most interesting and probably one of the most disgusting and frustrating of the ten curses God placed on Egypt. There were literally frogs into everything, and then Moses gave Pharaoh the power to choose. He could determine when the frogs would stop coming. He could decide how soon the frogs would have to leave. He could decide just when he would be able to sleep in a frogless king size bed! He decided quickly. What would you have chosen? If you could pick any time you wanted? As *soon* as you wanted it to stop? Amazingly, Pharaoh chose tomorrow! *Tomorrow*? Why in the world would he choose tomorrow? Why not today; as a matter of fact, why not right now—immediately. No more frogs, now! However, people choose to wait all the time. Tomorrow seems better. It seems more comfortable and less scary. Any other time seems better to many than right here, right now. The problem with that strategy is that all you really ever have is now. Tomorrow never really comes. Maybe Pharaoh had gotten used to his frogs. Maybe you've gotten used to your "frogs." You reason to yourself: "It might not be good, but at least it's comfortable." Pray for God to change your situation today. Go look for your miracle today. Go and find your answer *today*. Tomorrow never gets here and your frogs remain. He is ready now. Are you? There is no tomorrow.

Miracle Sightings and Spiritual Insights

Day Thirty-One

1 Kings 18:36–39

> At the time of sacrifice, the prophet Elijah stepped forward and prayed: "LORD, the God of Abraham, Isaac and Israel, let it be known today that you are God in Israel and that I am your servant and have done all these things at your command. Answer me, LORD, answer me, so these people will know that you, LORD, are God, and that you are turning their hearts back again."
>
> Then the fire of the LORD fell and burned up the sacrifice, the wood, the stones and the soil, and also licked up the water in the trench.
>
> When all the people saw this, they fell prostrate and cried, "The LORD, he is God! The LORD, he is God!"

Sometimes we need God to act in our lives in a public way for the benefit of others who are watching. God always uses our lives to affect other lives; it's just a matter of whether he uses a good or a bad example. Here, Elijah's faith and relationship with God were on display, and right in front of his enemies. *Nobody* was pulling for him. Nobody was praying for him. Nobody wished for him to succeed. But they needed to see his faith materialized and manifested—even if they didn't realize it. So God *moved.* Elijah would have never received this miracle if he hadn't had the faith to cry out to his Father in front of his detractors. Many times we offer "safe" prayers that are just between us and God—just in case he doesn't answer us, or in case the answer is "no." Safe prayers lead to a powerless life. When you put yourself out there and begin to proclaim what your God is going to do for you, well, now you're in miracle territory. When I don't care so much how I look in the situation, how it all affects me, what others think of me, or about my precious image or reputation, then I give the situation over to God and he gets all the glory. When *he* gets involved and takes over, then things begin to happen; things begin to change. When Elijah's enemies saw this miracle (fire from heaven), they fell down and exclaimed, "The Lord, he is God!" They weren't focused on the amazing prophet, but on his amazing God. Elijah got out of the way, and so can you. Do you have the courage to make one of your Impossible Prayers known to the world today? Share it with someone that you typically wouldn't. Call on God to show up, and then get out of the way.

Miracle Sightings and Spiritual Insights

_____

_____

_____

_____

_____

_____

_____

_____

_____

_____

Day Thirty-Two

Acts 7:55–60

> But Stephen, full of the Holy Spirit, looked up to heaven and saw the glory of God, and Jesus standing at the right hand of God. "Look," he said, "I see heaven open and the Son of Man standing at the right hand of God."
>
> At this they covered their ears and, yelling at the top of their voices, they all rushed at him, dragged him out of the city and began to stone him. Meanwhile, the witnesses laid their coats at the feet of a young man named Saul.
>
> While they were stoning him, Stephen prayed, "Lord Jesus, receive my spirit." Then he fell on his knees and cried out, "Lord, do not hold this sin against them." When he had said this, he fell asleep.

What an amazing man with an amazing legacy. His discipleship had made him so much like Jesus that he not only lived in much the same way but also died the same way: with compassion and conviction for the sake of others. Stephen had just preached one of the most powerful sermons recorded in history. He was calling out the religious hypocrites and speaking up for God when very few were willing to do so. Telling the truth had now gotten him into *big* trouble. However, he did not become bitter, but rather prayed for his enemies. In turn, God gave him a peek into his throne room. Stephen's eyes were opened and he saw Jesus *standing* at the right hand of God. As though saluting this great man of faith as he laid down his life for others. Wow! Now, you might have a hard time relating to Stephen, but I bet you can find an area of your life where you can identify with him. Have you taken a stand and it didn't work out as expected? Have you told the truth and only gotten in more trouble? Are you doing the right thing and it seems as though you now have more enemies or things have gotten worse? Take heart; Jesus stands for those who stand for him in the heat of the battle. Today I want you to *look* for an opportunity to take a stand for someone who cannot stand up for themselves. Look for a reason to stand up for the truth. Today, pray for great courage and then go out and watch for an opportunity to serve. It is now time for *action* in this forty-day quest. Take a stand.

Miracle Sightings and Spiritual Insights

Day Thirty-Three
Nehemiah 1:2–4

> Hanani, one of my brothers, came from Judah with some other men, and I questioned them about the Jewish remnant that had survived the exile, and also about Jerusalem.
>
> They said to me, "Those who survived the exile and are back in the province are in great trouble and disgrace. The wall of Jerusalem is broken down, and its gates have been burned with fire."
>
> When I heard these things, I sat down and wept. For some days I mourned and fasted and prayed before the God of heaven.

Nehemiah was a great leader. He was part of a great restoration and helped change the history of Israel. He was a visionary, a builder and a unifier... but what empowered and enabled him to become this great man was his heart for people. The condition of God's great city and the suffering of God's people moved Nehemiah to *action*. He didn't just feel bad; he didn't just complain about the problem; he didn't gossip or blame; he didn't excuse it or just put it out of his mind and wait for someone else to handle it. He took action and fasted for change. When was the last time you fasted and prayed for an "impossible" situation to change? There was no way that this problem was going fix itself. Someone was going to have to step up and "be the man" (or woman). Maybe there is a situation in your life that you are waiting for someone else to fix for you. Perhaps God is waiting on *you*. Maybe you're saying, "But I'm just not that sort of person. God doesn't use people like me." Really? Maybe you need to fast and pray for God to give you the heart of "that kind of person." Nehemiah changed everything for his people: their lives, their safety, their security and their future. But first he had to change himself—and only God could do that. The heart is a fascinating, mysterious, deep and vital place inside of us. It is the seat of our emotion and our will. Sometimes only God can change this part of us. And sometimes we need to rely on him like never before to perform the much-needed surgery. Fasting is a very effective way to *force* yourself to rely on him. Try it today, and pray for God to prepare to send you into a place with him that you have never been before—uncharted territory.

Miracle Sightings and Spiritual Insights

_____

_____

_____

_____

_____

_____

_____

_____

_____

_____

_____

Day Thirty-Four
Deuteronomy 3:23–25

> At that time I pleaded with the LORD: "Sovereign LORD, you have begun to show to your servant your greatness and your strong hand. For what god is there in heaven or on earth who can do the deeds and mighty works you do? Let me go over and see the good land beyond the Jordan—that fine hill country and Lebanon."

Moses wanted to go into the Promised Land. He had faithfully led God's people. He had put up with all of their arguing, complaining and bickering. He had mediated for them, intervened on their behalf, and suffered for them for forty years in the desert. Although he had not been perfect and he had made many mistakes, he had run a good race. Now he had one final request: "Please let me cross the Jordan River and die in the Promised Land." But God said "no." God had his reasons. As the perfect Father he always knows and does what is *best* for us. He can see everything laid out before him: past, present and future—all at once. He is not trapped in space and time; he created it. And he always answers our prayers. Always. Sometimes he says "yes." Sometimes he says "not yet." And sometimes, for reasons we can't always understand, he gently says "no." For over a month now we have been praying over our *Impossible Prayer List*. We have prayed, fasted, sometimes cried and then *looked* for God's answers. I want you to remember that sometimes the miracle is in the "no." We can't see the other side, but he can. Sometimes what is on the other side of that river will hurt us or be too much for us to handle at this time. I want to encourage you to continue to seek your miracles every day. Don't give up now. But also be very grateful for every answer, and continue to trust God. I'm sure Moses understands now what he couldn't see then. He's *got* you. Don't give up when he decides to withhold something that you don't need just yet.

Miracle Sightings and Spiritual Insights

Day Thirty-Five
Ephesians 3:14–21

> For this reason I kneel before the Father, from whom every family in heaven and on earth derives its name. I pray that out of his glorious riches he may strengthen you with power through his Spirit in your inner being, so that Christ may dwell in your hearts through faith. And I pray that you, being rooted and established in love, may have power, together with all the Lord's holy people, to grasp how wide and long and high and deep is the love of Christ, and to know this love that surpasses knowledge—that you may be filled to the measure of all the fullness of God.
>
> Now to him who is able to do immeasurably more than all we ask or imagine, according to his power that is at work within us, to him be glory in the church and in Christ Jesus throughout all generations, forever and ever! Amen.

What a powerful prayer from one of the all-time great prayer warriors! Paul wanted the Ephesians to truly understand who they were praying to. He prayed for them to have strength, power, deep roots, understanding, knowledge and all the fullness of God dwelling in their hearts through faith and love... and then he made a very important statement: This God of ours is *able* to do *immeasurably* more than we can even *imagine*. I want you to take off all caps, limits and ceilings today. Begin your day in meditation and let your imagination run wild! In your mind's eye, I want you to *see* all the good things that God could do for you. Go through your *Impossible*

Prayer List and just imagine all the different ways that God is in the process of answering those prayers. Be specific. Add color, smell and detail. Get out of your "box" for a moment and think of the endless possibilities, incredible opportunities, limitless potential, and infinite number of ways that God can put together a scenario for *your* miracle to arrive. He is not capped, limited or stuck in some box in which he must operate. He is free, and he is all-powerful, all-knowing, all-present, and eternally loving. Remember who you are talking to when you pray over these things today. You cannot even measure how much *more* he can do than what you have asked of him. So why not take it even higher? Push the limits of your faith. Dare to dream again. He is the ultimate dreamer. And he calls us to dream with him.

Miracle Sightings and Spiritual Insights

Week Five Discussion

Mark 8:22–26

They came to Bethsaida, and some people brought a blind man and begged Jesus to touch him. He took the blind man by the hand and led him outside the village. When he had spit on the man's eyes and put his hands on him, Jesus asked, "Do you see anything?"

He looked up and said, "I see people; they look like trees walking around."

Once more Jesus put his hands on the man's eyes. Then his eyes were opened, his sight was restored, and he saw everything clearly. Jesus sent him home, saying, "Don't even go into the village."

THE QUESTIONS OF JESUS

Week 5 Discussion: *"Do you see anything?"*

Once again, we find a man who desperately wants to see. It seems that this man had his vision at some point in his life. Perhaps it was an illness or an accident that took his eyesight from him, but he appears to have known what people and trees looked like from memory. This was his big chance to see Jesus for himself and he was taken to meet him.

Jesus took the man away from the crowd, which I believe is significant. Often Jesus healed people in front of spectators. Other times he healed people from a distance. But this time he led the man away, all by himself, for a very private interaction. Jesus was about to touch this man where it hurt. The source of his pain was probably whatever took his sight as a younger man.

The obvious question that jumps off the page is why did he require a second touch? Jesus had already put his hands on him and said, "Do you see anything?" To which the man replied, "I see people; they look like trees walking around." But then he gave the man a second touch. Why? Was Jesus having an off day? Did the man lack the faith that he needed to receive a healing?

I'm not sure why Jesus did it this way, but I do believe that sometimes we need a second touch. I know that I was thoroughly converted in 1989 when I made my good confession in the Chattahoochee River. However, twenty years later I needed him to touch me again. I needed him to heal some things inside that were left unhealed from my conversion. Some wounds are like that, they remain buried deep inside for years. Perhaps you need a second touch too. Let him do his good work, so that you can truly see.

Week Five Topics and Questions

- How has maintaining an attitude of gratitude and repenting quickly changed your prayer life?

- What have you seen God do in your life over the last five weeks?

- Discuss how eyes of faith see a situation differently than eyes of flesh.

- Discuss a curse from the past that you now see as a blessing. Bring to mind a time when God turned your mess into your message.

- Discuss why you think Jesus got so personal with this man when he spit on his eyes and put his hands on him. How has he gotten personal with you over the course of this project?

_____

_____

_____

_____

_____

_____

_____

_____

_____

_____

_____

_____

_____

_____

_____

_____

_____

_____

_____

_____

_____

_____

_____

_____

Pledge Six Reminder

6. When I am wrong, I will promptly admit it and quickly make amends.

This step is the way that I try to keep myself on track, so that I never have more than one or two bad days in a row. Have you ever been doing really well spiritually and you fall into temptation or blow it once again, only to be knocked off the beam and discouraged? That one day can lead to a bad week or even a bad month, and the enemy wins twice. First when you fall, but then he wins again by keeping you down and out of the game for as long as possible.

What if we develop the habit of repenting quickly and getting right back on the straight and narrow beam? I believe guilt is overrated and shame is not of God, but rather the work of the enemy. Guilt can be important and necessary as it leads me to feel bad about certain things I might do. Shame, on the other hand, is destructive as it causes me to feel bad about who I AM. Which one do you think comes from the Father? The reason I try to repent quickly is because I can't see the Father working in my life when my eyes are focused on myself. It's not that He stops working when I sin, but that I stop seeing His work when I am trapped in guilt and shame.

If need be, call a friend or trusted advisor and get help to see things clearly again. Repentance is rarely complicated, and most of the time the solution is quite simple. When I complicate things or stay in a state of "confusion" typically it is because I'm not ready to repent. Simply keep your side of the street clean, once again remove the scales from your eyes, and get back in the game. Timely repentance can actually become a healthy habit and you'll begin to realize that you are rarely tempted when you are searching for God and taking steps toward Him. Strongholds will be demolished as you keep things simple and continue to return quickly to the Way-Maker.

Day Thirty-Six
2 Corinthians 12:7b–10

> Therefore, in order to keep me from becoming conceited, I was given a thorn in my flesh, a messenger of Satan, to torment me. Three times I pleaded with the Lord to take it away from me. But he said to me, "My grace is sufficient for you, for my power is made perfect in weakness." Therefore I will boast all the more gladly about my weaknesses, so that Christ's power may rest on me. That is why, for Christ's sake, I delight in weaknesses, in insults, in hardships, in persecutions, in difficulties. For when I am weak, then I am strong.

Do you want amazing power to come into your life? Do you want an energy and enthusiasm that will draw miraculous results into your path? Do you want to go to another level and experience true breakthrough? Learn the secret that God revealed to Paul: the *power in weakness*. Paul fought against his "thorn" for what seemed like a long time for him—perhaps for years. He struggled with his sinful nature; he battled his shame; he wrestled with his own demons from his past; and everywhere he went there were constant "reminders" of his sin... then he figured something out. Boast in your weaknesses. Delight in your difficulties. Turn your shame into his glory. All the things that were once "curses" became *blessings* in Paul's life. He began to preach about his shortcomings as a way to glorify his Father. "If I can do it, then anyone can! Do you know who I once was, and who I still am?" He began to give God all the credit and claim only the mistakes as his own. And a new power came into his life. Today don't try to be perfect; just be yourself. Today, don't worry so much about what others think about you; worry about what *he* thinks about you. Today, share your weaknesses with others, but with no shame (guilt makes me feel bad for what I do, while shame makes me feel bad for who I *am*—guess which one isn't from God). You'll be amazed how people will be drawn to you. Delight in your weaknesses, insults, hardships, persecutions and difficulties. For when you are weak, then God is strong through you! Allow yourself to be weak and watch how power begins to flow back into your life. Now, pray that mighty prayer again.

Miracle Sightings and Spiritual Insights

_____

_____

_____

_____

_____

_____

_____

_____

_____

_____

_____

_____

_____

_____

Day Thirty-Seven

Acts 16:25–28

> About midnight Paul and Silas were praying and singing hymns to God, and the other prisoners were listening to them. Suddenly there was such a violent earthquake that the foundations of the prison were shaken. At once all the prison doors flew open, and everyone's chains came loose. The jailer woke up, and when he saw the prison doors open, he drew his sword and was about to kill himself because he thought the prisoners had escaped. But Paul shouted, "Don't harm yourself! We are all here!"

Paul and Silas were stuck, bound in stocks, in a dark, dank, stinking prison cell. They had done nothing to deserve being treated this way. As a matter of fact, they had done everything *right*. They were preaching the gospel. They were healing and driving out demons. They were being obedient to God. And now they were incarcerated? Why would God treat them this way? Why weren't things turning out right? They certainly deserved better. Where was God in all this? Do you ever feel this way? You have struggled, fought, suffered and obeyed, and *still* things have not gotten better. Maybe your circumstances haven't markedly improved over the last several weeks like you had planned. You wonder where your blessing is. Maybe this situation had nothing to do with Paul and Silas. Maybe it was all about the jailer and his family. It's hard to remember that, especially when we are in the heat of the battle or in the midst of the storm. Maybe your circumstances are not about you at all. Maybe there is a blessing for someone else in your perseverance. Try looking at your situation from a different angle. Let's view your circumstances through a different lens today. Maybe someone is going to see your persistence. Maybe they are watching and will see your deliverance. As someone once said, "You may be the closest thing to a Bible that someone else will ever read." Hang in there. Pray about it one more time. Get up again and do *not* quit. The ground is beginning to shake and the shackles are starting to loosen. Today is the day you will find your sign; today is the day for *your* jailbreak.

Miracle Sightings and Spiritual Insights

_____

_____

_____

_____

_____

_____

_____

_____

_____

_____

_____

_____

_____

Day Thirty-Eight
Luke 18:1–8a

> Then Jesus told his disciples a parable to show them that they should always pray and not give up. He said: "In a certain town there was a judge who neither feared God nor cared what people thought. And there was a widow in that town who kept coming to him with the plea, 'Grant me justice against my adversary.'
>
> "For some time he refused. But finally he said to himself, 'Even though I don't fear God or care what people think, yet because this widow keeps bothering me, I will see that she gets justice, so that she won't eventually come and attack me!'"
>
> And the Lord said, "Listen to what the unjust judge says. And will not God bring about justice for his chosen ones, who cry out to him day and night? Will he keep putting them off? I tell you, he will see that they get justice, and quickly."

Day and night she continued to ask. Day after day and month after month she pleaded. No one could talk her out of it, though many had tried. She *really* wanted this. She *needed* this. So she kept coming, and coming; and then she came back again. How bad do you want your miracle? Bad enough to continue? Bad enough to try again? Bad enough to hang in there when everyone else has given up? Even the "unjust" judge granted this woman her request. Even an evil man will relent and give in, if someone just refuses to give up. Someone who doesn't even care can be persuaded to capitulate if they are worn down by a relentless pursuer. Now, what about a just Judge, a righteous Father, and One who always cares? Do you not think that he will see that you get justice, and quickly? I know that it seems as if it has been a long time. I know that you have plenty of evidence to prove that he just doesn't work "like that" in your life or for people "like you." And I know that you are sometimes weary and discouraged. Remember: The light shines brightest in the darkness. The night is darkest right before the dawn. Keep on going to your Father. He *does* care. He is just. He will answer you. And before you reach for that comfortable excuse or that easy target to blame, while picking up the mantle of "victim" once again, hit your knees just one more time. This is your day; I can feel it. Go back to the Judge, who just so happens to be your Daddy.

Miracle Sightings and Spiritual Insights

_____

_____

_____

_____

_____

_____

_____

_____

_____

_____

_____

Day Thirty-Nine
1 Kings 3:7–14

> "Now, LORD my God, you have made your servant king in place of my father David. But I am only a little child and do not know how to carry out my duties. Your servant is here among the people you have chosen, a great people, too numerous to count or number. So give your servant a discerning heart to govern your people and to distinguish between right and wrong. For who is able to govern this great people of yours?"
>
> The Lord was pleased that Solomon had asked for this. So God said to him, "Since you have asked for this and not for long life or wealth for yourself, nor have asked for the death of your enemies, but for discernment in administering justice, I will do what you have asked. I will give you a wise and discerning heart, so that there will never have been anyone like you, nor will there ever be. Moreover, I will give you what you have not asked for— both wealth and honor—so that in your lifetime you will have no equal among kings. And if you walk in obedience to me and keep my decrees and commands as David your father did, I will give you a long life."

This was a life-changing prayer for Solomon. He didn't know it as he prayed, but *this* prayer would not only change his life but the destiny of an entire nation. He prayed for wisdom. He prayed for help in leading God's people. He prayed in humility and submission. He even seemed to surprise God with this request! God expected him to pray for wealth and long life and for the defeat of his enemies (he gets that all the time). And as we saw in the day devoted to Jabez, it's OK for you to do that. But here Solomon does something unexpected: He prays for wisdom sincerely, knowing that he doesn't have all that he needs to be the man that God has called him to be. Can you do that today? Can you sincerely and humbly ask God to provide you with *whatever* you need to be the man or woman that he intends for you to be? That means accepting even the tough times, the humbling circumstances, the refining fires and the necessary pain. Do you trust him completely to give you everything you need? Hopefully over the last month or so you have developed some new habits and a new mindset. A new trust should be emerging as well. Go ahead and ask God to do whatever it takes, and then look out! Maybe he'll surprise you the way that he surprised Solomon. Just maybe he'll give you what you need *and* what you want. Go ahead and give it a shot; what have you got to lose? He's waiting.

Miracle Sightings and Spiritual Insights

_____

_____

_____

_____

_____

_____

_____

_____

_____

Day Forty
Mark 5:35–42a

> While Jesus was still speaking, some people came from the house of Jairus, the synagogue leader. "Your daughter is dead," they said. "Why bother the teacher anymore?"
>
> Overhearing what they said, Jesus told him, "Don't be afraid; just believe."
>
> He did not let anyone follow him except Peter, James and John the brother of James. When they came to the home of the synagogue leader, Jesus saw a commotion, with people crying and wailing loudly. He went in and said to them, "Why all this commotion and wailing? The child is not dead but asleep." But they laughed at him.
>
> After he put them all out, he took the child's father and mother and the disciples who were with him, and went in where the child was. He took her by the hand and said to her, "Talitha koum!" (which means "Little girl, I say to you, get up!"). Immediately the girl stood up and began to walk around (she was twelve years old).

You have come to the end of the first *40 Days of Prayer*. I hope that you've found some miracles along the way and that you've begun to cross off some of your *Impossible Prayer List*. This is a program of progress, not perfection, so I hope you haven't gotten discouraged (you can always do it again with even more faith and effort!). But perhaps you are still waiting to see God *move*. Here we see Jesus faced with another "impossible" situation. The little girl was dead. No need to bother the Teacher anymore, because everybody knows when it's time to give up—and this was the time. Jairus was being tempted to give up, because everyone around him was telling him to quit and move on. They even laughed at the faith, or sight, that Jesus had when he told Jairus to believe. Everything comes down to what you believe to be true. For those who don't believe in miracles, it's very difficult to witness any. If you don't believe that God works miraculously anymore, or you think that he works but just not in a "biblical" way, then you will not see the power of God in the same way as someone with eyes of faith. It doesn't really matter what others think of your *Impossible Prayer List*; it just matters what *you* think. It doesn't matter what other people believe is or isn't possible in your life; it only matters what *you* believe. Notice how Jesus responds to the doubts and the laughter: He ignores them and keeps his eyes on Jairus. "Just believe, and you will see the power of God. Nothing is impossible for him; just trust me. Do *you* believe?" He is asking you. You need to decide what you think is impossible or too hard for the Lord. As for me? I've seen too much to doubt him. Anything is possible for him, and I mean *anything*. Now continue your journey of faith.

Miracle Sightings and Spiritual Insights

_____

_____

_____

_____

_____

Week Six Discussion

Week Six Topics and Questions

- It is time to review the first forty days of Impossible Prayers: What was the biggest epiphany, breakthrough or revelation that you experienced along this six-week journey?

- Share a specific answer to one of your Impossible Prayers and how you discovered it.

- Discuss ways that you can keep the spiritual momentum going from here.

Pledge Seven Reminder

7. I will deal with my doubts, excuses and complaints diligently and faithfully, and choose gratitude instead.

I have found that gratitude is the fertile soil in which miracles grow. However, complaining, excuse-making, and blaming choke my prayer life making it unfruitful. If I pay attention to the voice in my head as I go about my day, I can catch myself complaining about my circumstances, making excuses about my situation, and often trying to find someone else to blame for my lot in life. These are all weak and pathetic strategies for failure, and the recipe for a bitter prayer life.

So, I began to pay closer attention to my thoughts. I have discovered that self-talk is so important when it comes to creating the life that God has promised me. If left unattended, the brain can become our worst enemy and shipwreck the faith that God has given us. I have found that if I let my mind go wherever it wants to go it can take me into some very dark places. So I began to take seriously the scripture that commands me to "Take captive every thought and make it obedient to Christ." I found that it is not as difficult as it seems to control the voice in the head. It simply takes practice.

Many years ago God called me into prison ministry which absolutely changed the course of my life forever. One of the biggest things it did for me was give me a new perspective, a different viewpoint. At some point I always tell the men and women behind the wire, "I am quite aware that there are many of you in this room who would trade problems with me in a second if you were able." I believe the same to be true with many of you who are reading this book. Behind those walls I am always reminded that my life could be much different than it is today and probably should be because of the many poor choices I have made over the years. As a matter of fact if you ever ask me how I am doing, I will most likely reply: "Better than I deserve!"

Embrace gratitude today and hold it in your heart and in your mind. Your eyes will be opened and you will begin to see things as they are, through a new lens: a lens of FAITH. Pay attention to the signs and ask God to speak to you through His Spirit-- that still, quiet voice. You will find that He is fighting all around you, through you, and in you. And He is always speaking. Watch, pray, and listen, and prepare for your life to radically change.

Conclusion

Luke 8:42b–48

> As Jesus was on his way, the crowds almost crushed him. And a woman was there who had been subject to bleeding for twelve years, but no one could heal her. She came up behind him and touched the edge of his cloak, and immediately her bleeding stopped.
>
> "Who touched me?" Jesus asked.
>
> When they all denied it, Peter said, "Master, the people are crowding and pressing against you."
>
> But Jesus said, "Someone touched me; I know that power has gone out from me."
>
> Then the woman, seeing that she could not go unnoticed, came trembling and fell at his feet. In the presence of all the people, she told why she had touched him and how she had been instantly healed. Then he said to her, "Daughter, your faith has healed you. Go in peace."

This woman had been in a challenging, life-draining situation for twelve years. She had suffered, prayed and spent all she had on getting the help that she needed, and yet things got worse. Then she met Jesus. It was a "Hail-Mary pass." It was her last hope. He was the last house on the block. After this it was over. But then she met him. She reached out, and she touched him with faith. She held on, and that made all the difference. God *loves* great comebacks. I hope that is what has happened for you over the last six weeks of this project. We have reached out to him in faith and now we continue. It's time to hold on to the hem of his garment and not let go.

Congratulations on your spiritual breakthrough! If you have followed through on the steps, the studies and the daily journaling, then I am *sure* that you have seen some amazing things along this six-week journey. You have recorded very important evidence in your *Miracle Sightings and Spiritual Insights* journal. Perhaps God has given you much-needed resources, provided healing for your body or relationships, opened new doors for your career or personal life, or maybe he has "shown up" to rescue you in the midst of a fire, storm or wilderness wandering. I promise you that he has and will continue to answer you when you call, protect you as you go, and deliver you from all harm. Have you developed some new habits over the past forty days? Have tasks that used to be difficult gotten a little easier? Have you begun to notice things and *find* things that you used to pass by? Don't stop now. Keep up this very great and important soul work. Forty days is just a beginning. However, now you have some valuable momentum that can be of great advantage to you in your spiritual life. Or maybe you have been used to rescue someone else along their journey. Please continue to be that good example for them to follow.

Now is the time to make some new and fresh Impossible Prayers and continue to search and record daily. Share this forty-day challenge with a friend who might desperately need it. Pass on what you have been freely given. Let someone else borrow your faith at a time when theirs is weak. We all need help and we can all use some accountability in our spiritual life. Spiritual discipline will reap great rewards when it is combined with a childlike faith and great expectations. Continue this good fight and do not allow yourself to be discouraged. Keep your momentum by breaking the habits of complaining, excuse-making, blaming and quitting. Take responsibility *every* day and continue to call on our great God who is always listening, watching and working.

> Now to him who is able to do immeasurably more than all we ask or imagine, according to his power that is at work within us, to him be glory in the church and in Christ Jesus throughout all generations, forever and ever! Amen.
>
> —Ephesians 3:20–21

I wish you *all* the best in life. Perhaps we'll meet each other along the way on this journey of faith. Until then: Keep praying!

—Kit Cummings

As your Impossible Prayers are answered, post them publicly to encourage others to *believe* and participate!

My New Impossible Prayer List

1) _____

2) _____

3) _____

4) _____

5) _____

6) _____

7) _____

8) _____

9) _____

10) _____

"Have faith in God," Jesus answered. "Truly I tell you, if anyone says to this mountain, 'Go, throw yourself into the sea,' and does not doubt in their heart but believes that what they say will happen, it will be done for them. Therefore I tell you, whatever you ask for in prayer, believe that you have received it, and it will be yours. And when you stand praying, if you hold anything against anyone, forgive them, so that your Father in heaven may forgive you your sins."

—Mark 11:22–25

Let's continue moving some mountains...

About Kit Cummings

In 2010, Kit founded the Power of Peace Project. Using the experience he gained resolving conflict in some of the most dangerous areas in the world, he applies his principles to bring about change in prisons, schools, corporations, and the faith-based community. On MLK Day 2020, Kit was recognized by the NAACP receiving their Martin Luther King, Jr. *Living the Dream Award* for his contribution to civil rights, and his work with at-risk youth and prison reform. He was also appointed to the Georgia House of Representatives *Committee on Youth Gangs and Violence* in 2019, as part of Governor Kemp's initiative to reform prisons and eliminate youth gang violence.

Kit has been in over a hundred prisons, jails, detention centers and rehab facilities over the last decade and worked with over ten thousand prisoners and residents. He has journeyed on tours through Africa, Asia, Europe, and Latin America, and has negotiated peace between some of the most notorious gangs inside the U.S. prison system. He delivered an address about his powerful peace projects at the 2012 Gandhi Global Peace Summit in Durban, South Africa to representatives from the Gandhi, King, and Mandela families, as well as other iconic peacemakers from around the world, including the special assistant to the Dalai Lama. Kit has taken his *Forty Days to*

Freedom program into Cartel-controlled La Mesa prison in Tijuana, Mexico to work with men who are striving to be free, as well as working with addicts and at-risk youth in some of the toughest areas of that war-torn border city. Kit has planted seeds of peace all around the world.

Kit has authored six books, including the award-winning *Peace Behind the Wire, a Nonviolent Resolution* which has been endorsed by the King Family, and he also launched Power of Peace Radio. Kit also released *Protect the Dream,* which takes young people on a journey of character and leadership development designed to teach kids to dream big dreams and protect those dreams at all costs. The Power of Peace Project raises up much-needed positive role models in our schools and communities. What's next? Kit has now launched his POPP *Community Peace Initiative* in Selma, Alabama as he carries on Dr. King's Dream in that iconic and historic civil rights town.

Kit's latest book, *The New Convict Code*, flips the script on prison reform and aims to shatter the school to prison pipeline.

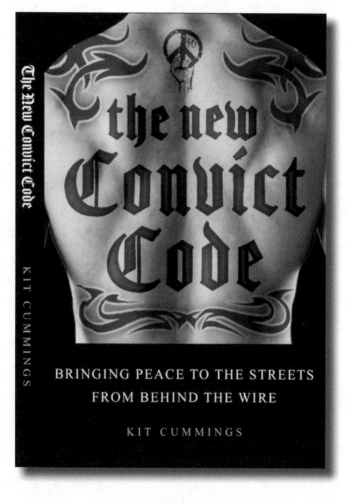

Available at
www.KitCummings.com

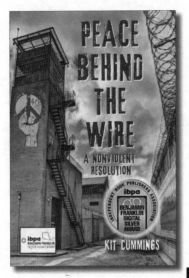

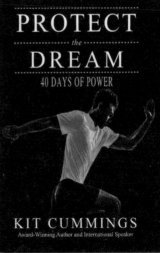

Available at
www.KitCummings.com